Odds, Sods and
Racing Certs

Odds, Sods and Racing Certs

Horse Laughs, Winning One-Liners
and Off-Beat Tales of the Turf

GRAHAM SHARPE

Robson Books

To dedicated punters who

'always break even' –

neither do I!

First published in Great Britain in 1996 by Robson Books Ltd,
Bolsover House, 5-6 Clipstone Street, London W1P 8LE

Copyright © 1996 Graham Sharpe
The right of Graham Sharpe to be identified as author of this work has
been asserted by him in accordance with the Copyright, Designs and
Patents Act 1988

British Library Cataloguing in Publication Data
A catalogue record for this title is available from the British Library

ISBN 1 86105 057 7

Printed by The Guernsey Press Company Limited, Guernsey,
Channel Islands

CONTENTS

FRANKLY MEMORABLE

Fall out from 'Magnificent Seven' Day, when Frankie Dettori rode all 7 winners at Ascot on September 28, 1996:

Lincolnshire cleaner Pat Epton backed all 7 of Frankie's winners – in 50p singles with no accumulator, winning just £19. The 59-year-old mum said 'What you haven't got, you don't miss.'

Anneley Yates told husband Darren not to waste £60 betting on Frankie's seven. The 30-year-old Morecambe joiner ignored her, and collected £550,000 from William Hill.

Even Frankie has some way to go to match US jockey Chris Antley, who rode 9 winners on October 31, 1987. He doubled up at Aqueduct and The Meadowlands and rode 14 horses in all.

There was only **one** Arkle.

Gordon Richards rode 12 consecutive winners between Oct 3-5, 1933 while Rhodesian jockey Peter Stroedel did likewise at Bulawayo in 1958 and jump rider Phil Tuck booted home 10 on the trot in September 1986.

Racegoers seeking investments for the future were spotted scouring rubbish bins for discarded racecards at the end of Frankie's record breaking Ascot day. Later, Frankie signed them – for a fiver a time, which went to charity.

For the first time ever BBC Radio 5 Live interrupted a reading of the classified football results to bring live commentary of Frankie's sixth winner.

The number of compensation claims for clothing spoiled by champagne stains following Frankie's bubbly-spraying celebrations after the seventh has yet to be revealed. Frankie's own 'Magnficent 7' turquoise underpants were later sold to salesman Ken Knott for £2500 at auction.

Frankie's previous best was six in one day on June 12, 1996, three each at Yarmouth and Kempton – and Fatefully figured on both days.

Dettori's BBC TV Sports Personality of the Year Awards odds were 100/1 immediately prior to racing on the day; 33/1 after his fourth winner went in, 8/1 when the last obliged; 6/4 a day later; 4/5 the day after that.

One lucky racegoer grabbed a piece of racing history when Dettori threw his goggles into the crowd after his last winner.

Spare a thought for *Sporting Life* writer David Ashforth who missed out on seeing history unfold when he stayed at home to mow the lawn instead.

Frankie Dettori, Philip Robinson and Jason Weaver were the **three** jockeys placed 1st, 2nd and 3rd in the 1996 2,000Gns who were all suspended for whip offences.

In 1982 Frankie's dad, Gianfranco, rode 6 consecutive winners at Milan – only to be beaten a short-head on the seventh.

James croft trained the first **four** runners home in the 23 runner 1822 St Leger.

# JOCKULAR REMARKS

'A genius in a saddle, lost out of one.' Capturing the essence of Lester Piggott, David Ashforth in his fine 1996 book, *A Punting Life*.

'He was kinda flopping about.' Phrase which somehow summed up the attitude of the Yanks to the Brits when used by American Jerry Bailey to describe the riding style of Walter Swinburn as the pair fought out the 1993 Breeders' Cup Classic.

'It's a lot tougher to get up in the mornings when you start wearing silk pajamas.' US jockey Eddie Arcaro explaining when he realized it was time to quit.

Michael Dickinson trained the first **five** home in the 11 runner Cheltenham Gold Cup of 1983.

'He told me that if I won on the horse I was down to ride at Ascot the next day I would be shot.' Peter Scudamore recalling an unpleasant late-night phone call.

'At his best he was the best – although he could be a horrible bastard to ride against.' Jockey Francis Woods on compatriot Tommy Carmody.

'If jobs were created for former riders, there would not be so many jockeys riding and, consequently, the ones that are riding would earn a better living.' David Hood, former jockey for Stan Mellor, turned PR man for bookies William Hill.

'Only one in a hundred knows how to use it – and only one in a thousand knows when to.' Former champion jockey Steve Donoghue on the whip, recalled by 93-year-old owner Frank Hill.

'Like a tart on a polo stick.' Amateur rider Jonny Greenall recalling the less than complimentary assessment of his riding by the late, great trainer Arthur

US Triple Crown winner, Citation, was **six** years old when becoming the first horse to pass $1 million in winnings in 1951.

Stephenson, a man whose own most frequently recalled quote was 'small fish are sweet' and who was so underwhelmed by his Cheltenham Gold Cup triumph with The Thinker in 1987 that he watched it on the TV at Hexham racecourse.

'It's all history now. Good luck to you all.' The entire text of Lester Piggott's speech at the 1996 Jockeys' Association Awards – now known colloquially as The Lesters in tribute to the Maestro – at which he received a special award. The speech brought the house down.

'If Ted Walsh retired, he would solve his nation's unemployment problems at a stroke.' *Independent* writer Richard Edmondson on Ireland's former champion amateur, also a commentator, columnist, trainer and horse dealer – could he be, by any chance, related to commentator, tipster, sometime jockey, columnist, synchronized swimming expert, interviewer – Derek Thompson?

'Keep riding slow horses and you'll be a slow jockey.' Recently retired Brian Rouse after he quit in 1996, who demonstrated his own speed of progress by riding his first winner in 1956 at Alexandra Palace – and his second at Chepstow, in 1972.

John Francome was champion jump jockey **seven** times.

'It still baffles people just how a young David Bowie look-alike with peroxide hair, driving a gold VW Beetle, ever landed a job with a man whose fashion starts and ends with cavalry twill and brogues.' Marcus Armytage on the partnership between jockey Anthony Tory and trainer Tim Forster – now which do you reckon had the peroxide hair?

'The phone never rings now. Trainers don't call so much and a few owners don't want me. You can't blame them. Who wants a 53-year-old jockey?' Maudlin reflection from former champ, Willie Carson who said during the same May 1996 *Sporting Life* interview, 'People take cocaine to get the buzz I get naturally. When I have won a race, I am as high as a kite.'

'Shutting the sauna door for the final time was a great relief.' Peter Scudamore on retirement.

'Bump, bump, thwack, bump, bump, thwack.' Description by an anonymous colleague of the *Life's* David Ashforth of Pat Eddery's riding style.

The first truly great horse, Eclipse, won all eighteen of his races in 1769 and 1770, **eight** of which were walk-overs as he frightened off potential opponents.

'I sometimes wonder if we put a bit more trust in a horse's eyesight than we should.' Richard Dunwoody on schooling in virtual darkness early on winter mornings.

'It seems slightly undignified to ring a trainer for a ride – it amounts to treading on another jockey's toes.' Gentlemanly, but disappearing, attitude from Tom Grantham explaining why he never had an agent.

'My money was invested in Wheeler's Restaurant and Jules's Bar in London.' But I doubt whether former hell-raiser and champion jump jockey Terry Biddlecombe meant that he had invested in shares in those establishments.

'I do not care a jot if jockeys fall off, and am rarely moved by stories that they have hurt themselves; they, after all, know what they are getting. When their horses are injured, though, it can cause the red mists to descend.' *Times* sports writer Mel Webb whose feel for the Sport of Kings was perhaps illustrated by his reaction to a trip to the races: 'I spent Saturday afternoon at the racing at Lingfield Park, and it felt more like a fortnight. The atmosphere? Easy. There was none.'

Nine runners contested the first Derby on May 4, 1780.

'Even my tights are a few milligrammes lighter than my usual pair.' Marcus Armytage on the rigours of making the weight for an important ride.

'We got as far as the third, and I broke my arm off him. We turned over the ditch and I got a kick from a following horse. But it was a heck of a buzz, I was sitting there holding my arm, thinking, "I wouldn't have missed this for the world."' Brendan Powell proving conclusively that while you don't have to be certifiably insane to be a jump jockey, it does give you the edge over the competition.

'The majority of flat jockeys are actually deformed. We're just small people.' So there is a soupçon of needle between jump and flat riders, to judge from the *Radio 5 Live* remark by Jamie Osborne in March 1996.

'When he sent me to England he gave me a million lire. At the time it was worth £366. He told me there was no more where that came from.' Frankie Dettori on father Gianfranco's tactics (successful) to make a man out of his son, who now realizes that 'In racing it helps to be a good bullshitter. You know you've made a mistake, so when they ask you about it you must have the ability to make excuses.'

On January 18, 1996, trainer Martin Pipe completed his **tenth** consecutive century of jump winners.

'Horses can feel you blinking . . . The difference between having a horse relaxed and having him run away is the edge of a razor blade.' Frankie Dettori.

'I would try every trick in the book. Bend the rules as far as they would go without actually breaking them. Kid anybody about anything. Looking back, I suppose I'm quite proud I played it that way.' Startling admission from the saint-like Peter Scudamore to the *Racing Post* in February 1996.

'I woke up and didn't fancy going to Plumpton.' Perfectly understandable reaction from 34-year-old Mark Perrett which caused him to quit there and then.

'I thought there was life after racing, but now I don't think there is.' The other side of retirement, illustrated by Keith Rutter, 14 months after he'd given the game up.

'They should be shot . . . When John Francome was at the top it took 70 or 80 [winners] to be champion. Now they're riding nearly 200 winners to be champion. So the percentage of rides has to go up. And where do they come from? From the struggling jockeys.' Jockey David Skyrme on the impact of jockeys' agents.

'Race riding is not a game. When you go out onto the racecourse, it's war.' Former top jump jockey turned top trainer Fred Winter, reported by Peter Scudamore.

'Some people seem more worried about horses being hit than they are about granny-mugging or child abuse. There is more cruelty going on around them in this country than there is on the racecourse.' Jockey George Duffield on the whip debate.

'The only way it will get more than a mile is in a horsebox.' Almost psychic comment by Ray Cochrane after he had ridden Taniyar for Reg Hollinshead in a 1½ mile race at Southwell – only for it to be revealed that Taniyar was in fact stable companion and sprinter, Loch Style. The incident happened in January 1996.

Trainer Michael Dickinson sent out a record **twelve** winners from 21 runners on Boxing Day, 1982.

'She was drawn too well for her own good.' Odd sort of excuse from Brian Rouse, explaining why his mount Stanerra could only manage sixth place in the 1983 Arc de Triomphe.

'I was worried about picking my stick up and losing the race in the stewards' room.' Jockey Ernie Johnson, who finished second in a tight tussle to the line in the 1972 Derby on Rheingold – compare and contrast with the following comment from another jockey in that same race: 'I wanted to get my horse's head past the post in front and then worry about the stewards.' Lester Piggott, who won that Derby on Roberto, driving his horse home ahead of Johnson's – and giving him a telling illustration of the difference in attitude which can separate the competent from the gifted.

'Jockeys ride to orders. If a horse is given an "easy" it's due to orders, don't always single out the jockey.' Michael Caulfield, Jockeys Association.

'I looked at Schumacher's obvious elation at becoming champion and I tried to work out why I had never felt like that. All I experienced was a sense of relief that the season was over.' Richard Dunwoody on becoming champion jump jockey.

Red Rum's trainer, Ginger McCain, saddled his first winner after **thirteen** years as a permit holder.

The smallest ever Derby winner, Daniel O'Rourke in 1852, stood just **fourteen** hands and three inches.

'I managed to do 10st 2lb the other day. I killed myself to do it. No other sportsmen are asked to perform regularly when they are not 100 per cent. We are. Nearly half of the top jockeys have to sweat hard to keep in the game.' A further Dunwoody insight into life at the top.

'I'm making plans to try to get hold of O J Simpson's lawyers but I don't think even they can help me in this one.' A chastened Willie Carson after being banned for a week after being caught on the line when easing up on odds-on Kamari at Lingfield, and failing to spot Major Dundee creeping up the inside to do him on the line.

'People should realize that racehorses only exist because they have been bred to race. They are man-made. They live in five-star luxury and if they weren't taught to race they would be no use to anyone and would have to face the bullet.' Willie Carson, to whom one might respond – the same could be said of jockeys!

1967 Arc de Triomphe winner, Saumarez,
returned the unusual odds of **fifteen** to one.

'Good trainers don't give you orders – it's bad trainers who give you orders.' Wisdom dispensed to Channel 4 viewers by Willie Carson.

'Who can forget the man upstairs. He has truly blessed me. He gave me some hands to communicate with these animals underneath me. So, on Easter Sunday, who can go without saying, "Thank you, Lord"?' Did you guess it was a Yank? Yes, Kent Desormeaux who, on Easter Sunday 1995, aged 25, became the youngest jockey ever to ride 3,000 winners.

'For anyone contemplating his future, the start of a steeplechase is not the place to be.' Peter Scudamore.

'I've had some stuff taken out of my head, but I don't think I really needed it.' Incredibly self-effacing comment from Declan Murphy whose dreadful race fall injuries nearly killed him.

'There's a lot of money in it, but it's so dull.' Jump jockey David Bridgwater on that other game, the flat.

In 1957 the Queen was the flat's leading owner, with **sixteen** horses winning thirty races for her worth £62,211.

'When I'm on my own I always play opera on my car cassette. But when I'm travelling with other jockeys I have to put up with pop groups like Dire Straits. You know the saying – "little things please . . .".' Jockey Mick Fitzgerald making sound sense.

'The highlight of the comeback was . . . to come back.' Classic comment from Lester Piggott who, in October 1995, also revealed the reason for his permanent (so far) retirement: 'I just haven't felt like making the effort to bring my weight down.'

'I was too small to be a window cleaner and too big to be a garden gnome.' Adrian Maguire on his career choice.

'You don't think about it. If you did, like racing, you couldn't do it. You can get killed crossing the road. Racing is more dangerous. You're dependent on a horse who could do anything, like break a leg at 40 mph.' Jockey Steve Williams on the comparative dangers of his other profession, boxing.

In 1976, Johanna Morgan became the first woman to compete in a British classic, riding Riot Helmet, 14th of **seventeen** in the Irish Derby.

'In racing, if something goes wrong, your next door neighbour will know before you tell him.' Jason Titley.

'I think they get paid too much money. A hell of a lot of jump races are won by halfway.' Former jump jockey Jeff King, taking a dim view of his current day counterparts including Richard Dunwoody: 'He likes it to look too nice', and Jamie Osborne: 'Talented, but a bit too much of a poser.'

'There is no point worrying about a fall. It will happen. The day you think it won't, it will.' Philosophical Jamie Osborne.

'One of the problems is that the people who protest most know least about the horses.' Statement not designed to appease Animal Rights Protesters from Jamie Osborne, a man who during the course of his career has been the target of a number of physical attacks from colleagues, amongst them Jenny Pitman. More of his homespun philosophy? Well, in 1995 he confided to a Sunday newspaper: 'At the end of the day which horse runs around a field faster is relatively unimportant.' Not, I suspect, though, to its owner and

The great Mill Reef, Derby and Arc winner, died in February 1996 aged **eighteen.**

trainer. And, somewhat ruefully, he reflected: 'Twenty years ago you could get pissed up every night, sweat it off in the Jermyn Street Baths and be champion jockey with 70 winners from fewer than 400 rides. The game is much more professional now.'

'Isn't it funny how much better horses jump when they don't have jockeys on their backs?' Observation from former Jump jockey Richard Pitman whilst commentating at Ascot in November 1995.

'Come on jockeys, line up – triers in front, non-triers behind.' Pre-stalls cry of now deceased starter, Capt Allison, recalled by Tim Fitzgeorge Parker.

'You could serve drinks on The Kid's back at the eighth pole and you wouldn't spill a drop before he hits the wire.' Colourful observation from anonymous racegoer on the smooth style of Steve Cauthen.

'I go in for an hour and a half in three thirty minute spells with a bucket of ice to stick my head in.' A bizarre image comes to mind of jockey Richard Hughes keeping his weight down in the sauna.

Jockey George Herring is said to have ridden **nineteen** consecutive winners during a career that ended when he died in a fall at Hull in 1796.

'The young Welshman would give himself a 50-50 chance after decapitation.' Tribute to the resilience of Carl Llewellyn by the *Independent*'s Richard Edmondson.

'I'm like a giggling schoolgirl if I have a glass of wine.' True confessions time from David Bridgwater in September 1995.

'Unfortunately it's the left collarbone. I couldn't have broken the other one as I've already had it removed.' Tough ain't the word for these chaps. Mick Fitzgerald shrugs – or at least half-shrugs off a problem injury.

'He eats virtually nothing, virtually all the time – something all top jockeys feel is a small price to pay to shine in their chosen sport.' Amanda Ursell on Frankie Dettori who, she says, rides at 8st 5lb when his natural weight is nearer 9st 10lb.

'My favourite hobby is playing paint ball. If you're timid it develops, and it has helped me develop initiative too.' Olivier Peslier – well, he is French, perhaps something was lost in the translation.

Mayonaise was the easiest ever 1,000 Guineas winner, with a **twenty** length victory in 1859.

'Everyone thought I was a four-stone better jockey two minutes after the race than I was two minutes before it.' Graham Bradley after winning the 1993 Martell Hurdle on Morley Street.

'It's really like going to school every day but without having any lessons to do.' Graham Bradley, on his profession.

'Asmussen never uses one word when 100 will do.' Jonathan Powell on US rider Cash Asmussen – who might spare some of those words to explain how he lost his given, if somewhat less glamorous, real name of Brian.

'Between being interviewed for the Racing Channel by Miriam Francome and winning the Arc de Triomphe on Lammtarra at Longchamp.' Frankie Dettori on his 'Most Memorable Sporting Experience', and before his Ascot Magnificent Seven.

Meteor, foaled in 1783, set a record for a British trained horse of **twenty-one** consecutive victories.

Lestor Piggott won on Scorpio in Bombay in February 1991 –
twenty-two years after his previous visit to India.

'I think jockeys should come with a health warning as far as marriage is concerned.' Richard Dunwoody.

'I expect that Piggott was offered a consideration for giving his consent.' Possible understatement of the century from Cadbury's PR man, Richard Frost, commenting on Lester's appearance in puppet-form in a TV ad for Cadbury's Creme Eggs.

'To the delight of the French racegoers Dick, after getting up and gesturing to the crowd, proceeded to relieve himself in the water jump.' Description of the actions of 1920s jockey Dick Rees after Easter Hero deposited him on the deck during the Grand Steeplechase de Paris, by Brian Lee, in his *Welsh Steeplechase Jockeys*.

'He was always turning up to give people lifts with an empty petrol tank. And if they didn't fill it up they never got anywhere.' Former trainer Helen Johnson Houghton, on Lester Piggott.

In 1856 Fisherman won **twenty-three** of the 33 races he contested.

'Any jockey can win on a great horse, but it takes a good jockey to lose on it.' Ernest Hemingway in *Men Without Women*.

'Just as Lester Piggott was described as the housewife's fancy, Alex Greaves should be the husband's flutter.' Nice idea, rotten tip from *The Times* on Derby day, 1996 – Alex finished last.

'They'd put a pair of knickers in your suit pocket and all hell would be let loose when you got home to the missus.' A chortling Jonjo O'Neill recalls the high-quality humour of the jockeys' changing room, going on to elaborate: 'They'd put a dead mouse in your shoe, cut the toes out of your socks, cut the front out of your pants, or undo the stitching around the arse of your trousers.' Deary me.

Popular handicapper Chaplins Club, who once won seven times in 18 days, won for the **twenty-fourth** time in July 1992 and was retired.

Once sold to gypsies for a case of whisky, 1980 Gold Cup winner Master
Smudge died in January, 1996, aged **twenty-five**.

 **FILLYFAX**

'Feminism is about equal pay, equal rights and throwing yourself under racehorses if needs must.' Julie Burchill, columnist.

'They used to try and bribe the lads. They used to go into the pubs and offer the lads money to say where I was. Extraordinary. If this is what they were like with me, I'm surprised Princess Diana hasn't hanged herself from a tree.' Jockey's wife, part-time model turned TV presenter, Miriam Francome on the media.

'I remember watching Elizabeth Taylor, and the whole idea of her chopping her hair off and pretending to be a jockey really fascinated me. I still watch it now whenever it comes on – that's a fact, it's not a fairytale.' Jenny Pitman on *National Velvet* – the mind boggles.

Sir Gordon Richards won a record **twenty-six** jockey championships, and is the only jockey knighted.

'For starters, she's a dandy brush short of a tool kit.' Marcus Armytage on British-born trainer in France, Deborah Camp-Simpson.

'I can think of plenty of male jockeys I could throw over my shoulder.' Gay Kelleway, dismissing criticism of female jockeys from their male counterparts – without giving away which of them she might wish to chuck over her desirable shoulder!

'John Dunlop and Paul Cole may be right in their assertions that girls are physically not suited to being jockeys. However, I console myself with the fact that I have a son coming up who knows very little about horses, but who is charming, tall and speaks slowly – obviously champion trainer material.' Perhaps with tongue ever so slightly in cheek, great supporter of lady jockeys, not least daughter Emma, Bill O'Gorman in a letter to the *Sporting Life*.

'Have you ever been embarrassed leading a horse round?' Rhetorical question from trainer's wife Deborah Evans, recalling the time she was responsible for trolling around lugging Samantha Fox's pride and joy, Touch Me, in her wake.

Frank Buckle rode **twenty-seven** classic winners from 1792, second only to Lester Piggott's thirty.

'Marjorie Orr, the *Daily Express* astrologer, is often my decision maker.' And what's wrong with Mystic Meg, Emma O'Gorman?

'Maybe in twenty years women will get the same opportunities as men.' Emma O'Gorman in the *Sporting Life*, March 1995 – only a few more years to go, then.

'Women trainers like Mary Reveley and Jenny Pitman have shown they can succeed alongside the men, but they won't give women jockeys a chance. Not even women want to stick by each other.' No honour amongst thieves, reports Lorna Vincent.

'Girls just don't get the chances. However many winners I ride, nobody takes note.' Apprentice Sarah Thompson, apparently not prepared even to consider that it could be because she is just another apprentice.

'Jockeys are the worst. I'd rather go out with a road sweeper.' Lady point-to-point champion jockey, Polly Curling, who added: 'Girls don't fall as well as men. Perhaps we're not built for it.'

Sir Gordon Richards rode in **twenty-eight** Derbies – winning in 1953 at the final attempt, on Pinza.

'I don't like women jockeys. I hope I never have to put up a lady rider.' Put-down from trainer and former biology teacher, Henrietta Knight.

'I sympathize with people who are addicted to drugs, because racing is a drug, you thrive on the adrenalin.' Gee Armytage, whose greatest claim to fame may well be that she is the only jockey on record to have had a sponsored bed.

'I know jockeys and trainers who are nearly bankrupt, but who still go on because they want to conquer. For a lot of us there are more bad days than good, but the good days are so good that they make up for the rest.' Gee Armytage.

'It stinks . . . That girl deserves an Oscar.' Chauvinistic fit of pique from John Reid after being relegated from first place in the Criterium di Roma at Rome's Capanelle, in favour of Jacqueline Freda on Try My Segnor, in May 1995.

The Hon George Lambton won 55 races with **twenty-nine** horses in 1912 to become leading flat trainer for the 3rd and final time with winnings of £22,884.

'I collect postcards of bottoms from all around the world. They're all stuck up around the kitchen.' Well, what can you say to that? Trainer Kim Bailey's wife, Tracey.

'She often comes to watch the telly in the ladies' changing room and her language is even worse than mine.' Polly Curling on Jenny Pitman.

'He might marry me now he's seen what I can do.' Fledgeling trainer Julie Craze after fiancée Stuart Webster had ridden her first winner, Queens Check.

'I keep seeing this jockey, or that trainer, being asked for opinions by various commissions and boards, and they're all male. I don't think I've ever been accepted and I don't suppose I ever will be.' Jenny Pitman. Doesn't that just sum up the blinkered attitude of too many sections of the racing world?

'I used to crave, really crave, a tomato or a grape. It became too much in the end.' Gay Kelleway on why she packed in riding and moved on to other things, including tipping for the *Daily Sport* newspaper, before becoming a trainer.

'It is beyond belief that there are still so many bastards in charge of horses in 1990s Britain.' Less than rosy-spectacled view of veteran horse welfare campaigner, Vivien McIrvine.

'Time after time, my children are treated as unwelcome aliens at the races and, by association, so am I.' Trainer Jacquie Doyle with one of the reasons why the average age of racegoers seems to be rising.

'I was brought up in racing and I've known the score for a long time. If you come in thinking that you're going to make a big difference you're going to be greatly disillusioned.' One of the few women in racing to have made any sort of impact, Alex Greaves, speaking, one hopes, without disillusionment.

'This is the only sport in which women compete against men on equal terms and you have to be better than a man to get the opportunity to prove it.' Jockey Diane Clay.

1965 Grand National winner, Jay Trump, was put down aged **thirty-one** in August 1988.

RACEY CHARACTERS

'On that rare occasion in the stands when your horse hits the front, all sorts of wonderful things happen – there is an adrenalin surge, a feeling of idiotic brotherhood with all the other gifted souls who have picked the same one and a sense that you have predicted something, controlled a small piece of the world.' Horse-racing specializing modern artist, Mark Wallinger, on the joys of backing a winner.

'I have still not given up my dream of owning, training or riding an Aintree Grand National winner.' Former Monkee turned winning jockey, Davy Jones, whose 1996 victory in a small race boasting prize money of £2,968.35 produced the memorable comment from writer Peter Corrigan: 'If you pay peanuts you get Monkees.'

Jockey Steve Cauthen wed Amy Rothfuss when he was **thirty-two**.

'One of Kipling's female characters complained once that kissing a man without a moustache was like eating an egg without the salt. Horse racing without betting would be much the same to me.' Old salt Robin Oakley, Political Editor of the BBC.

'If you've still got a few quid to spare at the end of a day's racing, go and buy a bottle of champagne.' Sound advice from David Gower, former England cricket captain.

'Just backing a horse, whether it wins or not, is enough to add a certain tingle to the whole racing experience from paddock to finish.' TV weather forecaster, Sian Lloyd.

'The attitude that owners should not need to make it [racing] pay is simply archaic. That sort of "landed gentry" philosophy should have gone out of favour hundreds of years ago.' Sports promotor Barry Hearn, whose wife breeds horses, who won nearly £40,000 by backing his first horse Charming Charles and who seemingly doesn't like certain bookies: 'Abolish off-course bookmakers – High Street betting shops cannot really be justified.'

Born in 1906, Billy Nevett rode 2068 British winners in **thirty-three** seasons.

'I followed his career right from the start, went to Kempton four or five years in a row to watch him run in the King George VI chase on Boxing Day and even had my photograph taken with him. He was fantastic, everything you could want in a race horse.' Desert Orchid groupie, golfer Laura Davies.

'He was a bad winner. Losing was his thing. And God knows, he lost.' Fellow *Bilko* star, actor Mickey Freeman, on how Phil Silvers punted on racing – unsuccessfully as Silvers himself once admitted, confirming that his cash 'slipped into the bookies' hands as if it was magnetized'.

'I have the odd flutter now and then. The last bet I had obliged in a four runner race at 5/1. It was most welcome but now I think I'll quit when I'm ahead.' Terry Venables after backing a tip supplied by Brough Scott.

'There's no buzz like going racing. It's just unique. You get fights at football matches, but people do thousands having a single bet on course and just walk away unruffled.' Jimmy Pursey, lead singer of punk group Sham 69.

The biggest ever Derby field was in 1862 when **thirty-four** went to post.

'If I put a proper bet down, I'll put a copy of the *Racing Post* under my left foot and stand on it during the race. Most of the time it never works but the odd winner has made it a habit with me . . . I'll always rate horse racing above rugby. There's absolutely no comparison, especially when it's a big meeting. Give me the thrill of Cheltenham to Twickenham any day.' Former England Rugby Union star, Stuart Barnes.

'You've just got to hope you spend around £12,000 and get lucky. I certainly wouldn't spend more than that. I can teach people about comedy, I know about that. But I can't pick out horses so I get the experts to do that.' Jimmy Tarbuck on the strategy which has bought him a number of winning horses.

'It was 1971 or 1972. Lester [Piggott] had a ride in the Grand Prix de Deauville. He said "Have something on that, it can't lose." I played £20,000 to win. It came last . . . I don't like to travel to go racing. If you lose money it can make the two-hour journey home torture.' Actor Omar Sharif.

On May 1, 1996, beting shops celebrated their **thirty-fifth** anniversary.

'I've never put a bet on in my life.' Actor Bill Tarmey trying to live down the gambling-mad character of his alter-ego, Jack Duckworth of *Coronation Street*. Perhaps he should take notice of fellow *Street* star, Charlie Lawson, alias Jim McDonald, who says he bets for 'the excitement of winning. There's a great feeling cheering home winners at a racecourse . . . We go racing for the horses and the crack. We should never computerize and monopolize racing. It will rip the soul out of it.' Incidentally, Lawson is a founder member of the National Association for the Protection of Punters.

'Having an occasional punt is probably my only vice and I do enjoy it. Racing is all about opinions, and trying to beat the bookmaker in a calculated and methodical way is practically a science in itself.' Racehorse owner and occasional snooker player, Peter Ebdon.

'I was ten and my grandmother was the street's bookie's runner. I used to pick one out virtually every day and come home to have the bet with my dinner money. It was quite a regular occurrence for me to get back from school to find Nan being carted off in the Black Maria.' West Ham manager Harry Redknapp.

Celebrated today by a race at York, great 18th century horse, Gimcrack, winner of 26 of his **thirty-six** races, never won at York.

'If he were a horse he'd be put to sleep.' Alan Ball on his former England team-mate, the arthritis-stricken Mick Channon.

'I wouldn't have my house if it wasn't for Cois Na Tine. The house is a shrine to him. There are no football pictures up; just racing pictures.' Manchester City and Republic of Ireland footballer, Niall Quinn, whose house is named after his Group 3 winner, who was later sold for a hefty price (and profit) to America. Quinn, who later bought his equine hero back again to ensure a happy retirement, is planning a second career running syndicate horses 'for a group of people who are doing it for fun. People who, should it not work out, won't get hurt.'

'Surely, the only reason one has a bet is to win. I think there are few things more satisfying in life than backing a winner.' Home Secretary Michael Howard talking to *Sporting Life* Weekender's John O'Hara.

Gary Carter and Willie Ryan rode **thirty-seven** winners apiece to be joint champion apprentices in 1985.

Sixty seven victories by **thirty-eight** horses, to the value of £22,949 made Nicky Henderson 1986-87 champion jump trainer.

RIGHT ROYAL RACING

'That is the first time she has had fourteen hands between her legs.' John Francome's observation upon watching the Duchess of York contesting a marathon horse race in the Qatar Desert on The Morning Line.

'I was absolutely delighted, Ma'am.' Which was probably not quite what the Queen Mother wanted to hear from jockey Dave Dick after she asked him how he felt when he saw her own Devon Loch fall on the Grand National run-in, thus enabling Dick on ESB to surge past for victory in the 1956 race.

'If a horse is owned by the Queen or George Smith or me, it is the trainer's name that is always attached to the horse . . . The poor owner is not going to be mentioned at all in the whole story. He is only there to pay the bills, and to be told where the horse will run . . . I tried and tried to alter this and, really, I just gave

---

78 year old Scobie Breasley landed the Barbados Cockspur Gold Cup for the third consecutive year in 1993 when Chou-Chou Royale won at **thirty-nine** to one.

up.' A miffed Sheikh Mohammed expressing frustration at a trait all too commonly observed in trainers, who believe they have an unimpeachable right to be regarded as the guardians of the horse-flesh in their care, regardless of the feelings of the true owners.

'I will excuse the fact that he beat the horse I put my money on by a very short head.' Prince Charles preparing to present the trophy to jockey Pat Hyland after the 1985 Melbourne Cup.

'If you see Sheikh Mohammed in the winner's enclosure, he just about forces a smile. But if there are Irish winners or a syndicate in there, they're whooping and hollering and laughing. That's what racing should be about.' But possibly not what Royalty should be about! Chris Spencer-Phillips of the Racehorse Owners' Association.

'It's one of the real sports that's left to us: a bit of danger and a bit of excitement, and the horses, which are the best thing in the world.' The Queen Mum sums up her love of the turf.

Colombian jockey in Italy, Augustin Herrera, was banned for **forty** days after being discovered using a battery powered device in May 1996.

'If you were to place a bet now you would probably get odds of about 1000/1. But you never know your luck.' Sandringham stud manager Michael Oswald on the horse which could just win the 1998 Derby and break the Queen's duck in the race. The bay colt, born there in spring 1996, is a son of 1978 Derby winner, Shirley Heights, and grandson of the great Mill Reef. Mum is the useful Abbey Strand. As we went to press the colt was un-named. Remember, if it does win the Derby – you heard it here first.

Frank Durr-trained Spark Chief exceeded **forty-one** mph in 1983 when setting the fastest electronically recorded 5f time of 53.7s at Epsom.

OWNER UP

'People say sailing is an expensive sport, but to own a racehorse is the equivalent of burning a yacht on the front lawn every year.' *Sunday Telegraph* writer Adam Nicolson, who added: 'This is the world where cash is king but chance is queen.'

'A brilliant performance on the day will always be a brilliant performance. A horse's inability to repeat it, often for physical reasons, does not diminish his early achievement.' Peter Savill, owner of Celtic Swing, a prime victim of the build 'em up and knock 'em down school of journalism.

'Don't buy a horse. It's all expense and worry.' Answer from racehorse owner and MD of race sponsors, Thresher, Jerry Walton, in response to the question: 'What's The Best Advice You Ever Had?' He was then asked 'And The Worst?' and answered: 'Don't buy a horse. Because when you have had a winner it is one of the best feelings in the world.'

Forty-two runners set off in the 1928 Grand National – only two completed the course.

'You cannot take out a donkey and bring him back a racehorse.' Sheikh Mohammed on the effect of a winter in Dubai on Godolphin inmates.

'If you haven't got the balls to do it you shouldn't be let in at the last minute.' Robert Sangster condemning plans to allow 'wild card' entry to the Derby for horses which were not originally entered.

'I always wear the same pair of lucky boxer shorts when the old boy runs . . . it is getting such a routine that they could walk to the track on their own.' Paul Matthews, owner of Cheltenham Gold Cup winner, Master Oats.

'If ever I wanted to wish anyone ill, I would wish that they won with their first horse on its first run. That gets you thinking the game is dead easy – it isn't.' 76-year-old veteran owner of 200 winners, company boss Jack Joseph.

US jockey Ed Carvalho was still an apprentice when he rode his first winner in 1993 – at the age of **forty-three**.

'I met with Sheikh Mohammed and we came to a sort of mutual agreement, although not a great truce in the sense that "I won't bid against you if you don't bid against me."' Robert Sangster on how he and the Sheikh managed to put a stop to the auction duels which forced the price of many yearlings sky-high.

'I'm successful because I'm brilliant and I'm wealthy because I'm successful.' Owner Bill Gredley, whose wealth has been estimated at £80 million, forgets how important his modesty has been.

'We had grown to love him and I can honestly say I can't remember ever having been so upset about anything before or since.' Dr Desmond Morris on the death of his first racehorse Son Of A Gunner.

'This was planned back in March and now you know why the ceremony was timed for 6pm rather than 3pm. Now at least we shall be able to pay for half the champagne.' Just married Peter Savill after his Raphane was backed from 9/4 to even money and won at the Curragh just hours before he wed Ruth Pinder on 25 May 1996.

Ernie Piggott won his third and final jump jockey title with **forty-four** winners in 1915.

SADDLED WITH SEX

'Turning a racehorse into a stallion is not merely a matter of chucking a copy of the *Kama Sutra* into his box and saying, "Go get 'em, boy."' Bloodstock writer Sue Montgomery informing readers of *Inside Racing* that becoming a stud does have its complications.

'I've fallen in love with my horse. It's a safer bet.' Actress Sharon Stone – neigh, lass.

'I've looked at plenty of other women, but never another jockey.' Trainer Sir Mark Prescott on stable rider George Duffield, with whom he has always enjoyed a good relationship.

'The object of it all, surely, is to cause smiles of delight, rather than the sniggers of disbelief that trailed in the wake of the brazen and foolish who dressed as if they

He had his first ride in nineteen **forty-five** and didn't stop until 1991 when he was 69. US jock Willie Clark clocked up 1143 winners.

were on their way to an orgy.' *Daily Telegraph* fashion writer Hilary Alexander on the stylish at Royal Ascot 1994.

'If you want to ride for me, you haven't a chance unless you come over to my place and sleep with me and the owner tonight.' Jockey Vicki Haigh, recalling the invitation from an anonymous trainer to whom her response was: 'I'd rather die.'

'Corbière and I have even been to a stag night together. He behaved impeccably.' Jenny Pitman on a night out escorted by a Grand National winner.

'He, like all the others, had manners enough to let Miss Oliver cut out the running.' Marcus Armytage recalling Anthony Tory's participation in a hurdles race at Stratford in which lady jockey Jacquie Oliver 'split her breeches from backside to breakfast time'.

'Sexy Samantha Coles, 21, used to own a horse. Saddley, the lass had to sell it when she became a model. Neigh bother, Sam, you'll always stirrup a lot

---

Riding in England for the first time, in July 1992 at Redcar, the world's top female jockey, Julie Krone, scored a **forty-six** to one treble.

of interest on Page Three. Any foal knows that.'
Thoroughbred caption to topless shot of attractive filly
gracing Page Three of the *Sun* on 16 April 1996, and
headed Long May She Rein!

'I've always had my knockers, and I've still got them.'
Slightly confusing confession from 1996 Lady Jockey of
the Year, Alex Greaves, as she accepted the honour at
the 'Lesters', the Jockeys' Association Annual Dinner.

'What a great idea it would be to have a Page Three
National – we could have Page Three girls jumping
over fences topless. And I could be one of the fences.'
Wishful-thinking comments attributed to John
McCririck by the *Daily Sport* on Grand National Day
1996. Surely such a campaigner for women's rights
could never have thought, let alone uttered, such
sentiments.

'I'd love to take a naked Page Three girl round the
course on my back.' Bizarre ambition revealed by
jockey Guy Lewis prior to his Grand National ride on
Brackenfield in 1996 and after he had been pictured by
the *Daily Sport* newspaper on hands and knees (fully
clothed, fortunately) being straddled by a less than
fully-clothed topless model, Rachel Travis.

Thoroughbred, Charter, won a bizarre **forty-seven** mile race in 1825 in
Russia between two Cossack horses and two English racehorses.

'I haven't enjoyed nine [some reports said twelve] minutes so much for a long time. Sex is an anti-climax after this.' Jockey Mick Fitzgerald after winning the 1996 Grand National on Rough Quest, speaking without reckoning on the consequences to fiancée Jackie Brackenbury whose response was: 'He's never lasted twelve minutes in his life.' Presumably the three-minute difference is accounted for by the time spent milling around at the start – although how that could have been better than sex is beyond me!

'He said to me the other day, "Gosh, you looked at me then as if you loved me." I said, "I do, I do." I adore him, but I'm happier not living with him.' Model and trainer's assistant Miriam Francome on estranged husband John.

'It's hard to have a conversation with many of them. They only talk about two things, and one of them is horses and the rest has a double meaning.' Jockey cum model Victoria Haigh on her weighing room counterparts in a *Loaded* interview in February 1996, during which she was asked whether she would model for unclad shots and replied: 'I would do if Lichfield was the photographer. I like nude pictures.'

Dick Saunders became the oldest winning Grand National jockey in 1982, partnering Grittar to victory at the age of **forty-eight**.

'We'll be asking the chief executive of Channel 4 to have Mr McCririck removed as we consider him to be past his sell-by date. We are also asking our members to write to all female MPs to draw their attention to the fact that Mr McCririck is chauvinistic towards women, who represent about 25 per cent of our customer-base.' Warwick Bartlett, Chairman of the British Betting Offices Association, not happy about Big Mac's performances on C4's *Morning Line* – and eliciting the following response from the man himself, seemingly unrepentant as ever. 'If Warwick Bartlett wishes to draw up a petition to get me sacked by C4 Racing, then he will be swamped by people eager to add their signatures. I have to agree that Warwick Bartlett has caught the public mood and is on to a sure-fire winner.' That was in February 1996 – he is still in office as these words are penned.

'It wasn't the wife.' Stable lad Bob Mason to the female doctor examining him after his charge, the much-hyped Celtic Swing, had bitten him – and left the teeth marks to prove it – in a somewhat sensitive spot.

'That black book is playing havoc with our sex life.' Trainer Lucinda Russell's boyfriend, Magnus Nicholson, complaining to the *Sporting Life* in February 1996 that she spends her spare time reading *Timeform* every night.

'Frankie asked my permission to ask if he could marry Catherine on Friday night, the engagement was on Saturday, party on Sunday, and headache today.' Father of champion jockey Frankie Dettori's wife to be, Catherine Allen, Professor Twink Allen, recalling their engagement timetable.

🏇

'I think it's hilarious when these funny little guys make rude suggestions to me. They only come up to my navel and I always feel like I'm their mother.' The Amazonian, 5ft 10in jockey cum model Vicky Haigh, this time pouring her heart out to the *Daily Star*. No wonder her male counterparts don't seem to have too many complimentary things to say about Ms Haigh, who went on to reveal: 'Trying to get a race when you're a woman is hard enough. Trying to get a race when you've been to bed with owners and trainers is impossible,' she added a further insight: 'Women can't win in this game. If they sleep around they're tarts and laughed at. If they don't sleep around they're just laughed at.' Surely she isn't unhealthily obsessed with the subject?

🏇

'He's everything I'm not. He's young, he's beautiful, he has lots of hair, he's fast, he's durable, he has a large bank account, and his entire sex life is ahead of him.' Envious sportswriter Si Burick contemplating the future for American equine idol Secretariat, 1973 US triple crown winner.

'I am an incredibly bad loser. I wail, scream, lie on the floor and indulge in what people must think is a bizarre sexual ritual. It is so shaming I have cut down on my visits.' Portly actor Richard Griffiths, who must startle the horses if he always reacts in that manner when failing to back a winner.

'I fell at the first in the Grand National last year [1995] and the horse trod on my private parts. I was being attended by a St John Ambulance person, and at ground level I saw that the feet were stockinged. At first I was more concerned with my painful predicament but as I started to look upwards I realized I was being helped by a man dressed as a woman – wearing lipstick and the full monty.' Jockey Mick Fitzgerald, relating the tale of a gay at the races.

'It's a standing joke between me and my staff that the minimum bet is inversely proportionate to the woman's chest size. If I see an ugly bag in the distance I'll say minimum bet of £20 for her, but if it's a dolly bird she can have 10p any time.' And one wonders how on-course bookie Stephen Little might react if a woman bookie sized him up in a slightly different way, whilst deciding what amount of bet to accept from him.

'The last time they opened a stand at York my colleague John Oaksey described it as "Major Leslie Petch's erection" which was very flattering to Major Petch.' Sir Clement Freud on York's new Ebor stand.

'I can still picture her vividly. She was in red undies and looked fabulous.' Carl Llewellyn crediting *Sun* Page Three girl Angela Lee as the inspiration behind his victory on San Giorgio at Worcester in September 1995.

'I get a lot of love letters, but they're mainly from men between 70 and 90 years old. I might take one up and disappear to Barbados. But it won't be the bloke who sent pictures of himself in compromising positions.' Jenny Pitman who was also heard to remark during 1995 of one of her favourite horses: 'Willsford – the only Willy I enjoy seeing every day.'

Lionel Holliday set a record of **fifty-two** winners in a season
for a British breeder in 1954

'When I arrive at Channel 4 on a Saturday the lads expect me to have slept with six women the night before, and another two that same morning.' John Francome.

'A great advertisement for sex twice a week. She was covered by Magic Ring early on in the season but didn't get in foal and so she was covered again on Sunday and Tuesday.' And on the Saturday, David-Chappell-trained Thatcherella scored again, winning a May 1996 sprint handicap at Newbury.

In 1957 Doug Smith won at Lingfield, Brighton and Wolverhampton but drew a blank at Longchamp, all within the space of **fifty-three** hours.

HORSE DROPPINGS

'Hucknall's a prat! The race should be renamed The Dickhead Hurdle.' The *Daily Star* becoming hot under the collar in an Editorial Comment column in February 1996, condemning pop mega-star Mick Hucknall of Simply Red for refusing to permit Newton Abbot to name a race the Simply Red Handicap Hurdle.

'I went to the Cheltenham Festival once, but never again. For someone as fat as me, it's impossible. I would like to see more generous sanitary arrangements.' An extreme example of recent criticisms of Cheltenham for squeezing in more racegoers than the course can adequately accommodate. This from comfortably proportioned actor and racing enthusiast, Richard Griffiths.

Foaled in 1874, Hungarian bred mare, Kincsem, won all **fifty-four** of her races in six different countries.

'I would be a most unpatriotic judge if I did not accede to this request.' Judge Esmonde Smyth who postponed a hearing at his Irish civil court in February 1996 – so that witnesses could attend the Cheltenham Festival.

'So addicted to the sport that he even reads John Francome's racing thrillers.' Writer Will Buckley on jockey Carl Llewellyn. Will, a man so keen on a wager that he placed his wedding list with bookmakers William Hill, rather than the traditional big store, was spot-on in this instance. I speak as one who has ploughed through the Francome catalogue. As ever, though, the 'Greatest Jockey', is well aware of his own shortcomings, commenting: 'If I wasn't John Francome, the former champion jockey, I would have been wiped out in one year.'

'One of our owners, Berys Connop, took some hairs from his chest and sent them off to a faith healer – and the horse hasn't looked back since.' Sarah Hollinshead, discussing the unorthodox cure for her trainer father Reg's In The Money, who won two races in spring 1996. Was that form worth taking at faith value?

Aussie sprinter, Schillaci, set a record for 1000 metres, clocking a time of **fifty-five** seconds in 1993.

'I think more of this horse than my wife as I ride him all the time at home, rounding up the cows.' Trainer John Manners in January 1996 after his Killeshin had won at Taunton, and who also told reporters: 'I've forgotten my false teeth, so don't ask me many questions.'

'I certainly don't think we'll be seeing a zorse winning the Gold Cup at Cheltenham this year.' Simon Clare of the BHB, reacting to reports in early 1996 that experimental breeders have successfully crossed a zebra with a horse, thus producing a zorse, which they plan eventually to race.

'I don't know why I'm called Peter – always have been.' Not so surprising that trainer Miles Henry Easterby should be unaware of the derivation of the name by which he is invariably known – after all, he doesn't even know his own birth date – he says it's 4 August, but according to his wife his birth certificate says 5 August!

Puerto Rican horse, Camarero, won a world record **fifty-six** consecutive races between 1953 and 1955.

You won't be too surprised to learn that there are **fifty-seven** separate bets in a Heinz.

'People said I could not win with this horse. If he fails, I say, that's because I'm a brick-layer. If he wins, it's because I'm a farmer.' We can only speculate on the precise meaning of this monologue from Cwmbran trainer Ivor Jones, whose 7/1 shot Tilt Tech flyer had just won at Newton Abbot, prompting his bizarre comment.

'He has appeared to win races at both Nottingham and Windsor this season but lost out each time – because he has a short neck.' What a fantastic excuse! The horse's neck was too short – classic of the genre, revealed in May 1996, by trainer Stan Mellor, on behalf of his Court Nap.

'Why was it a slow time? Because we went too fast.' A masterpiece of warped logic by Willie Carson, desperate to explain the defeat he had just suffered on a fancied joint favourite at Newmarket in April 1996.

'All I want out of life is a cigar, to see a bullfight and have the freedom to turn up the heating when I want to.' Trainer Sir Mark Prescott's rather modest life wish-list.

The largest ever field for a flat race was the **fifty-eight** who turned out for the 1948 Lincoln.

'I'm dying to get on the programme and would love a pop at that bloke they call Hunter. They might bill me as Sparrow.' Jockey David Bridgwater revealing a likely-to-remain-unfulfilled ambition to appear on TV's *Gladiators*.

'Everybody talks about him as if he has found a cure for cancer, brought about complete peace on Earth, scored the winner in the Cup Final, and dated Marilyn Monroe in his lifetime.' And *didn't* Peter O'Sullevan achieve all those things as suggested by jealous *Sporting Life* hack Bruce Millington?

'Fortunately, the horse dropped out of contention at the second last and I was able to hang up and concentrate on not getting eaten.' Owner Peter Savill recalling listening to a race commentary from Sedgefield via a long-distance phonecall, whilst on safari amongst lions in South Africa.

'I'd like to get a grey in there, and a three-legged horse if possible.' Derby supremo Edward Gillespie sounding somewhat desperate about his role of reviving interest in the self-styled greatest horse race in the world, which one might have thought would not need gimmicks.

'She was working in a circus, posing for people to throw knives at her, performing on a trapeze, doing back-flips while standing astride two horses. Maybe that is where I get my agility from or some people might say that explains my behaviour, that underneath it all I'm a clown.' Frankie 'Coco' Dettori on his mother.

'One doesn't want to go to school, one doesn't want to make his bed, one doesn't want to brush his teeth, one doesn't want to do his homework.' What was *he* on? Former top jockey Angel Cordero, who became a trainer at the age of 53 in 1996, but apparently believed he was running a nursery.

'Colonel Bill (Whitbread) died in November 1994 and so he will not be at Sandown this year.' Press release straight out of the School of Stating the Bleeding Obvious, put out on behalf of 1996's 40th anniversary of the Whitbread Gold Cup sponsorship.

'They're all the same until they race – dangerous at both ends and uncomfortable in the middle.' Novice owner Des Lynam, having become part of the Motcombs Club Syndicate, owners of the Neville-Callaghan-trained Pat-Eddery-bred two-year-old,

Sixty winners gave Tim Moloney the first of his five jump jockey titles in 1948-49.

Motcombs Club. Watch out for riotous times here after trainer Callaghan admitted to the *Observer* in April 1996, 'Discipline has not been my strongest point, and obeying the law has never been my number one priority.'

'Four flat jockeys who wouldn't eat much.' Parsimonious, or what? Editor of *Wisden,* and racing fan, Matthew Engel, invited to select four sporting figures for a mythical dinner party. The man can be forgiven, though – having made the following comment about Ireland: 'A country where the boat-race course would be considered good to firm.'

'Congratulations. With the winnings you'll now be able to afford some long trousers for your next visit to my racecourse.' Reported comments of Chairman of Clairefontaine racecourse, Pierre Lepeudry, to short-panted trainer Charlie Brooks, after his Padre Mio won there in August 1995.

'If brains were a virus, jockeys would be the healthiest people in the country.' Trainer Philip Mitchell.

US trainer William Johnson won with **sixty-one** of the sixty three runners he sent out in 1807-08.

'Trying to go racing without paying is a national pastime. We suspect we are losing £2m in revenue.' Morag Gray of the Racecourse Association, and after a friend told me how he made a fortune simply by standing near an unattended gate and letting people through for a few quid a time, with no one paying the slightest attention to what was going on, I can well believe it.

'Any man who has to save up to go racing has no right to be on a racecourse.' Jeffrey Bernard of the *Spectator.*

'Miles and miles of bugger all.' Description of Newmarket recalled by Robin Oakley in the *Spectator,* who also informed readers that 'the perfect filly, one racing sage used to say, should have the head of a lady and the behind of a cook.' – not Keith Floyd's, though, we trust.

'Walter has not been sacked, it is just that his retainer is not going to be renewed.' Weasel words from a 'spokesperson', explaining why Walter 'Choirboy' Swinburn's services were being dispensed with by the Maktoum camp.

Just **sixty-two** victories were sufficient to land the jockeys title for Steve Donoghue in 1915.

'It's like having a quisling in your country.' Outraged reaction of owner Tony Richards, 30 years a box-holder at Royal Ascot, upon discovering that the course's caterers Letheby & Christopher had removed British beef from the menu during the Mad Cow scare of 1996 – claiming that they had been forced into the decision by other box-holders' requests.

'The tongue-strap is a nylon tight – nylon tights don't come loose unless you want them to!' Trainer Val Ward refuting claims that a loose tongue-strap had misled the judge in a Southwell photo-finish in May 1996.

'The groom rests his hand on the flank of Whistlejacket, to reassure or to comfort. Stubbs has concentrated much feeling in that hand placed on horseflesh. This is English painting's truest equivalent to the creating hand of God the Father, reaching out to spark life into Adam on the ceiling of Michelangelo's Sistine Chapel.' And there was me believing that artist George Stubbs' 18th-century life-size work, 'Whistlejacket and Two Other Stallions with Simon Cobb, the Groom', was just a nice picture of a racehorse. Critic Andrew Graham-Dixon reveals the hidden depths of the work.

Noel Murless sent out 33 horses to win **sixty-three** races, worth £66,542, in 1948 to become leading flat trainer for the first of nine occasions.

'The *Daily Star* AWT 1m 2f challenge Series Handicap Qualifier Division One – now, isn't that a race title to conjure with. It evokes all the magic of Lingfield.' *Sporting Life* writer, John Santer, in sarky mood.

'In a curious way the overt dishonesty makes it straighter; if everyone knows what's going on then it's fair cheating all round.' Matthew Engel, editor of *Wisden,* attending a flapping meeting at Llangadog in Wales in April 1996.

'Just like a slave; my papers were bought for £500.' Paul Kelleway on becoming an apprentice with Harry Wragg at the age of fourteen.

'The Youth of America ignore horse-racing. And why shouldn't they, for horse-racing is ignoring the youth of America.' *Sporting Life* American Update column. And, from the same paper, a fascinating revelation by Alan Shuback shortly before Her Majesty the Queen preferred a trip to the Derby to opening the biggest sporting occasion in the UK for many years, Euro 96: 'No American President, or even a candidate for the presidency, would dare to show his face at a racetrack these days. It is just too politically incorrect an activity for a politician of national stature in which to engage himself.'

'It is quite possible that we will one day have a racehorse who's by a rat out of a pig and may even be a bit of a dog.' Paul Haigh speculating on advances in genetic development and the news that male sperm could be produced by mice.

LOSERS

Judy Higby – who boasts the all-time hard-luck story. She woke up on the morning of Grand National day 1993 with an odd feeling that for some reason the day's big race would not go ahead as planned. She visited her local bookie in Tring, Richard Halling, and asked him to quote odds that she was right. He thought he was doing her a favour by declining. Fortunately she didn't get on the phone to me – I'd have offered 1000/1. And, of course, the botched false start resulted in the race being declared void.

The Gobbler was to have been the somewhat risqué name of a Richard-Hannon-trained two-year-old, until Jockey Club officials stepped in to guard our morals. He was re-named Golden Ace.

Wolfie – the poor horse who had to take the strain when 18-stone comedian donned racing silks and clambered aboard to promote a new video.

The largest ever Grand National field was in 1929
when **sixty-six** went to post.

The Grand National – which placed just ninth in a 1996 BMRB survey of '10 Events People Want to See Live on TV' – finishing behind such contests as Wimbledon, the Winter Olympics and the Commonwealth Games.

Aldaniti, the Grand National winner, looked a real gift horse in the mouth when he crunched up and ate a Polo mint – which turned out to be a promotional gold one, worth a cool £1,000.

Betty's Hot Shot, the fictitious horse 'owned' by Jack Duckworth's syndicate in *Coronation Street*, enjoyed a pretty dismal career under its motley band of owners – one crazy soap fan even tried to stick £50 on it to win a non-existent race. Sympathetic Corals refused the wager.

The waitress with racecourse caterers Letheby & Christopher who was removed from a hospitality box at Chepstow – because the un-named host objected to her spotty complexion.

Sixty-eight winners gave Stan Mellor the first of three jump jockey titles in 1959-60.

John McCririck features in a video film played to patrons of the Paramount Bar in Bon Accord Street, Aberdeen. It is located actually *in* the bar's Gents' toilets where it can be studied and watered at the same time.

Herman Blake, ridden by Jill Dawson at the 1992 Badsworth point-to-point meeting, tragically collapsed and died, only to suffer the further indignity of being posthumously disqualified by stewards.

Ascot racecourse officials were made redundant in 1995, and further salt was rubbed into their wounds when one revealed: 'We aren't even getting compensation for our bowlers, even though we paid for them.'

Graham Bradley was snoring through 40 winks – when he should have been partnering Charlie Brooks' Macedonas at Worcester during 1995. By the time he awoke Simon McNeill had stepped in and won on the horse.

In his first year as leading owner on the flat, 1985, Sheik Mohammed had **sixty-nine** winning horses.

Frankie Dettori, Philip Robinson and Jason Weaver finished first, second and third in the 1996 2,000 Guineas on Mark of Esteem, Even Top and Bijou D'Inde, only to secure unwanted notoriety as, for the first time ever in a Classic, the three placed jockeys were all suspended for misuse of the whip.

Sean McCarthy became the first jockey in Britain to test positive for drugs after his urine sample was found to contain cannabis and speed. In October 1995 he lost his licence for two months.

Sporting Index, a spread-betting company, were widely pilloried for offering punters the chance to bet on the outcome of the infamous O J Simpson trial in October 1995.

Gary Hind, who had just finished eighth on The Deaconess at Nottingham in October 1995, was the target of such a strident verbal attack from the owner's husband, Michael Clarke, that it attracted the attention of the stewards, who found Clarke guilty of improper conduct on the racecourse and fined him £275.

Rider of eight St Leger winners, **seventy** year old John Jackson died in 1839.

The Ambulance at Brighton racecourse caused an accident to a spectator in October 1995, when it failed to negotiate a bend and ploughed through the rails, hitting a middle-aged racegoer who had to be taken to hospital although he was later released.

Boxing Match, running in a race at Fontwell in May 1995, acquired a unique form line – 'Weakening when hit streaker, pulled up' – after 29-year-old Stephen Brighton shed his clothes and ran on to the course, into Rodney Farrant's mount's path.

Stephen Davis earned himself a £75 fine after carrying and waving about a yellow plastic bag during a hunter chase at Hereford in April 1995. The object of the exercise was to persuade 10-year-old Articflow to put his best foot forward. It didn't work – they finished fifth – perhaps the horse was a bag of nerves.

Wear The Fox Hat was deemed to be an offensive or suggestive name by the Jockey Club who, in March 1995, refused to permit the two-year-old to run until its name was changed – to Nameless.

Julie Krone rode **seventy-two** winners in 59 racing days at
Gulfstream Park, US, in 1992.

Steve Smith Eccles faced an unusual obstacle during a chase at Uttoxeter in October 1984 – when a racegoer threw a dustbin at the jockey and his mount Green Dollar. Unsurprisingly their performance proved to be a load of rubbish, and they failed to win.

Ciaran O'Neill became the loser of all losers when he failed to win a walkover at Blankney's point-to-point meeting in April 1994. O'Neill and Mister Chippendale duly completed the walkover – only for O'Neill to be disqualified for failing to weigh in.

However, there was a precedent – or three – for this oddity. Terry Smith failed to win a walkover at Tweseldon point-to-point in May 1990 when the horse bolted and couldn't be brought to the start in time.

In 1935 in Panama Raoul Espinoza rode a horse in a walkover, only to weigh in 4lb light.

And then there was Trelawny – gifted with a walkover for Royal Ascot's 1964 Queen Alexandra Stakes, for which he was the only horse declared. But the entire day's racing was rained off. So it was rescheduled for the Saturday – and it was rained off again.

Hans Waltl, an Austrian, experienced the equivalent of 'Come in number ten your time's up' when he was ordered to pull up his mount, Simon, in a tannoy

Known as the emperor of trainers, Robert Robson died aged **seventy-three** in 1838, with 34 classic victories to his credit.

announcement by the stewards at the Braes of Derwent point-to-point in April 1994, after the pair had refused twice at the second fence and again at the third, fourth and eighth – and then been lapped by the rest of the field.

Frank Passero, a Florida trainer, denied malpractice with regard to the alleged misuse of 'Fiery Jack', a substance containing cayenne pepper. In March 1996 the authorities accused 62-year-old Passero of applying, or allowing someone else to apply, the substance to the genitals and rectum of his horses to make them run faster – well, wouldn't you, under those circumstances? The trainer, denying the charges, admitted that he used Fiery Jack but, he said, only therapeutically.

A spectator at the 1996 Cheltenham Festival needed eight stitches to a head wound – after being hit on the head by a pair of shoes, tossed over a balcony by a celebrating party of Irish racegoers.

A trainer at a Gosford, Australia, country meeting in February 1996, was observed leading his runner for the next race down to the betting ring. He was

Tony McCoy landed a record **seventy-four** wins in his first British season, 1994-95 to be leading conditional rider.

eventually persuaded that his runner didn't really need to see what odds were being chalked up for his chances, and was diverted back to the parade ring. The local stewards then fined the trainer for being 'drunk in charge of his racehorse'.

Bookies William Hill were only too keen to help promote the race being run at Kempton on Monday, 6 May 1996, in aid of an establishment for dyslexics. Which made it all the more unfortunate that their betting odds in their *Racing Post* advertisement appeared under the heading 'Dyslexia Institutite Handicap.' I soopose it kan hoppen to ennywun.

Mary Bogle, 26, was looking forward to a romantic honeymoon in exotic climes when she wed 32-year-old bookie Ronnie Bogle in August 1994 – only to find herself standing next to him in the York betting ring – still wearing her wedding dress. 'Ronnie said he wanted to do the race meetings at York and Chester,' explained Mary. 'But I said the only way I was going along was if I wore my wedding dress. This is my honeymoon, after all.'

Credited with making the Kentucky Derby one of the world's great races, Col Matt J Winn, who died aged 88 in 1949, watched the first **seventy-five** runnings of the race.

Vic Rail, 49, an Australian trainer, died tragically in September 1994, of circumstances resembling a plot from an episode of *The X Files*. Scientists believed that Rail had been struck down by the same mysterious virus that claimed the lives of 14 horses – 12 from Rail's own stables – during an outbreak of a pneumonia-type illness. Scientists said that the virus appeared to have mutated so as to become virulent to both humans and horses, which is very rare.

Some horses just can't be trusted. After 85 consecutive defeats, Gussie Mae raced over 7 furlongs at Atlantic City in June 1995, needing just one more failure to set a brand-new turf record of the least successful horse of all time. Wouldn't you just know it, the Kandace Affa-owned runner led from start to finish to clock up his debut victory – and leave previous record holder Really A Tenor still the holder of at least half a record, unenviable though it may be.

True love didn't run smooth at a Cleethorpes betting shop when punters complained that customer Howard True was stinking the place out. Garlic fan Howard eats six cloves of the highly regarded substance each day to help cure a chest condition and admits the aroma tends to linger, but argued 'If everyone ate garlic we'd all be a lot healthier and no one would notice the smell.' But bookies Ladbrokes banned 47-year-old Howard from all their local branches and commented in January 1994: 'We have to take account of the majority.'

Newly installed closed-circuit security cameras at Newcastle and Kelso were stolen in October 1994. Said the Jockey Club spokesman David Pipe, with commendable restraint: 'It is very unfortunate.'

Six days before landing the biggest victory of his life on Royal Athlete in the 1995 Grand National, jockey Jason Titley was locked in a linen cupboard at London's Hilton Hotel by fellow riders after feeling tired and emotional whilst attending a racing award ceremony.

A circus was banned from Epsom, home of the Derby, because it featured horses. The local council would not permit the Cottle Sisters Circus to perform in the area in January 1994 because, said Recreation

---

Bob Davies and Terry Biddlecombe shared the jump jockey's title in 1968-69 with **seventy-seven** winners apiece.

Committee Chairman Eber Kington, 'The council took the view that it did not wish to see horses performing unnaturally on its land.'

'We find it unbelievable that we have been banned from Epsom, whose only claim to fame is horses,' said Gerry Cottle.

If you're sceptical about mystic Meg, then what would you think about a winner-finding system which involves mind-reading? A Hertfordshire company called Probex Ltd launched a 'proven wealth creation package' called SELECTA in 1995. Its literature declared: 'The SELECTA is based upon the fact that more than half of a list of expert journalists show a profit every year and if you have the ability to read their minds you must be able to show bigger profits.'

Thank you, I've heard enough – I'd prefer to stick with the novel methods of another tipping service which advertised in the *Sporting Life* in March 1995, promoting an Isiris Racing of North Seaton service called Losers, which boasted that its last four selections were all unplaced. It also featured a glowing testimonial from 'A S of Hull' who gushed: 'I'm making good profits too by backing against your losers.'

Jockey Tommy Lowrey, who rode Airbourne to win the 1946 Derby, died aged **seventy-nine** in January 1991.

Steaks from failed racehorses are the chef's speciality at a restaurant in Warsaw, Poland. *Daily Star* readers were informed in January 1995 that 'customers are even told the names of the nags they are eating when their meals are served'. I can imagine disgruntled punters on their way home from the races nipping in to eat the favourite they've just done their boots on.

Sporting Life editor Mike Gallemore gave his newly purchased horse a mint – the ungrateful nag promptly bit him on the nose – plastic surgery was necessary to repair the damage.

Former jump jockey Mark Caswell regaled *Sporting Life* readers with the tale of how jockey Paul Carvill lost a finger in an accident with his reins. He was rushed to hospital, followed by his digit, which had been located by fellow rider John Suthern, who arrived at the hospital and turned round to pick up the finger which he had left on the back seat – only to see his pet dog 'licking his lips in appreciation as he finished off the final morsel'.

Trainer, Joe Carr, whose Lochranza won 27 races for him, died aged **eighty** in May 1996.

WINNING CERTS

105-year-old Rosie Hamburger was appointed as the *New York Post's* latest racing tipster during spring 1996. She started betting, boasted the paper, 'sometime before World War One'. Sadly, she expired later in the year – but her final selection was a winner.

Edinburgh bookie Victor Gold allowed hard-up punter Iain Hunter, a butcher hit by the Mad Cow scare of 1996, to stake six steaks – worth £20 – on his Grand National tip – Rough Quest, the winner. Victor must have been mad.

750 smoking enthusiasts attended a specially arranged race meeting at Meadowlands Racetrack in the States, hosted by *Cigar Aficionado* magazine. They saw the last race won by – Light It Up.

Elnathan Flatman was the first ever champion flat jockey, riding **eighty-one** winners in 1846.

Tote employee Sally Anne Thomas of Maidstone stunned her bosses by appearing topless in the *Daily Sport* after pledging that she'd rather dispense with clothes altogether than wear the official Tote uniform.

Trainer Howie Tesher from Florida was the first to introduce nasal plasters – as popularized by footballers and ruby players – to horses, equipping five-year-old Porto Varas with the breathing aid.

John McCririck made a spectacle of himself – officially –winning the 1996 Spectacle Wearer of the Year Award.

Nottingham Forest goalkeeper Mark Crossley launched a telephone tipping line during the 1995-6 soccer season, 'to pass on to callers the benefit of inside information he gets from contacts in the racing world'. Wonder if he made a net profit?

Retired Aussie racehorse Subzero, the 1992 Melbourne Cup winner, made public appearances entertaining the crowds by literally taking a bow.

Joe Dillon, who won the 1903 Irish Derby on Lord Rossmore, died at the age of **eighty-two** in July 1967.

A joker caused consternation to air passengers arriving at Los Angeles by putting a sign on the roof of the Hollywood Park racetrack reading 'Welcome To Chicago'.

A recently discovered 45-second film of the 1895 Derby, probably the oldest piece of British film extant, was valued at over £10,000.

Called up before Australian stewards to explain the improved performance of two of her runners at a Queensland track during 1996, trainer Tania Geisel declared it was because they had had a chat with American Krista Cantrell – who claims she can talk to animals.

Equine nappies for racehorses were invented by Sydney trainer Anthony Cummings, who said, 'They mean less mucking out'.

Kiwi Dr William Allen became the first professor of racehorse breeding after Cambridge University named him their Professor of Equine Reproduction.

Five times Cheltenham Gold Cup winner Golden Miller's first victory, at Leicester in 1931, was worth **eighty-three** pounds.

A five-year-old jumper, Sir Turtle, became the first horse sponsored by a government tourist office, courtesy of the Cayman Islands Department of Tourism.

The Black Death Vodka Chase at Haydock and *The Voice* Newspaper Adonis Juvenile Novices Hurdle at Kempton were two of the more unusual sponsored races run on 24 February 1996.

Sixty-two-year-old veteran US trainer Frank Passero ran up a 7,000,000/1 sequence of fourteen consecutive winners in an 11-day streak at Gulfstream Park beginning on 24 January 1996, at winning odds ranging from 3/5 to 11/1.

Lester Piggott and Gordon Richards were the only racing figures featured in *The Greatest*, a book by Daley Thompson purporting to examine the careers of 100 British sports-people.

A trophy presented to Sir Gordon Richards was stolen in 1956 and was retrieved from a TSB vault in 1991.

Former Epsom trainer Ted Smyth died in April, 1996, aged **eighty-four**.

Racegoers were somewhat surprised when 87-year-old Frank Hill turned up at Brighton races in October 1970 to see his Saysana win – as the *Daily Telegraph* had just printed his obituary.

Josh Gifford and Peter Scudamore have both claimed the wicket of cricketing-great Brian Lara. Gifford bowled him during a 1991 charity match and Scudamore caught him during a similar event in 1992.

Coronation Street was one of the sources from which Frankie Dettori learned to speak English.

Sixteen-year-old jockey Riccardo Cangiano rode six winners from eight mounts at Florence on 21 May, 1995 – when he had previously ridden just seven winners in his entire career.

When Graham Bradley woke up too late to partner Champion Hurdle favourite Alderbrook in a schooling session he was sacked from his position as the horse's jockey. He was later taken on to ride Collier Bay for Jim Old – and the combination stormed to victory in

the 1996 Champion Hurdle, beating into second place
. . . Alderbrook.

When Ben Dearg won a 2-mile chase at
Wolverhampton in February 1971 he went down in
racing history as the first horse ever to be returned at
the decimal odds of 13/10.

Former Monkee pop star, Davy Jones, sported a beard
as he achieved a lifetime ambition by riding Digpast, a
50th birthday present from daughter Sarah, to win the
Amateur Riders' race at Lingfield in February 1996.

Windsor's 0990-11-11-45 Royal Star and Garter Chase
in November 1995 was the first race ever to feature a
telephone number in its title. It related to a refuge for
disabled servicemen.

Aiden O'Brien set Irish racing alight during 1995.
Amongst his feats were running up a sequence of
winners on 23 consecutive racing days, and sending
out four of the first five home (first, second, fourth and
fifth) in the 29-runner Tattersalls Stakes at the Curragh.

Former jockey Billy Parvin, who rode in 16 consecutive Grand Nationals
but never won, died in 1991 aged **eighty-six**.

Jockey Ralph Neves was thrown from his mount into wooden railings at Bay Meadows, California, and the track doctor pronounced him dead. Taken to the morgue, a doctor injected adrenalin into his heart, whereupon he arose 'half-conscious and wearing but one boot and blooded riding pants'. He staggered to a cab stand and returned to the track where he wanted to ride out the rest of the card! This incident occurred in May 1936 and Neves survived until 1995, when he died again, aged 74.

Jason Brautigam sponsored a race at Lingfield in order to ask his girlfriend to marry him. The Zoe Hurworth Will You Marry Me? Stakes was run on 4 March, 1995 – and she said . . . yes.

David-Nicholson-trained Moorcroft Boy, who broke his neck in a fall at the 1994 Becher Chase at Aintree, made an amazing comeback to win the 1996 Scottish Grand National at Ayr. Just as heartening was the story of Raahin, who actually died for six minutes whilst being operated on for knee problems in 1994 – only to return and win at Fontwell for former jockey Ron Atkins.

Racing fans with a spare £3,000 were offered the opportunity of buying the head of Lester Piggott – well, a bronze bust of the legend by leading sculptor Helen Cox, in a limited edition of thirty (the number of Classic winners he rode). They became available during early 1996 and were reportedly selling well, although I doubt whether the subject splashed out for one.

Convicted drug trafficker Chim Shing-Shung, serving an eight-year sentence in Hong Kong, went to the High Court in November 1995 to declare that the prison's practice of removing the racing section from inmates' newspapers (to reduce the instances of illegal gambling, claimed the authorities) amounted to a violation of human rights. Judge Raymond Sears, presumably a racing fan, accepted the argument and ruled in Chim's favour.

Georgia Sandown Cragg earned her unusual middle name – by being born in that racecourse's car park when she arrived too quickly in January 1996 as Mum and Dad, Paul, and Debbie, headed for hospital. The racecourse responded by giving the infant honorary life membership.

Jack O'Donoghue's last runner as a trainer, Myjinka, was a winner for him in January 1996, when he retired aged **eighty-eight**.

22-year-old rider Amanda Pluckett nearly lost an ear after it was sliced off by a horse's hoof when she fell during a point-to-point chase at Barbary Castle, Wiltshire in January 1996. It was reattached by surgeons using 20 leeches to relieve blood pressure as its veins reconnected themselves. I wonder what Luca Cumani, so fond of referring to bookmakers as leeches, thinks of that?

American superhorse Unbridled's Song, beaten favourite in the 1996 Kentucky Derby, was the first horse ever to have his own pages on the Internet: (http://www.napanet.net/unbridledssong/). And a human counterpart is English rails bookie Bob Stock who, in April 1996, became the first on-course bookmaker on the web – http://ourworld.compuserve.com/homepages/Bob Stock. And talking of the web, *Sporting Life* Weekender writer, Malcolm Heyhoe, experienced one with a difference when he visited his local betting shop in May 1996: 'What should I see but a punter perched on a stool, with a tarantula on his shoulder . . . I watched a couple of races on SIS then left. As I stepped into the street the punter was holding the tarantula in the palm of his hand, the pair of them peering at the form of a handicap hurdle.'

Steve Donoghue and Charlie Elliott shared the 1923 jockey championship with **eighty-nine** winners each.

Roads in and around the village of Ballydehob in south-west Ireland are closed off annually to allow a racing programme, of six events from one to two miles, to take place.

Isle of Skye punter Brian Wiltshire was refused a bet by his bookie because his bank account was short of cash. The horse won and he should have collected over £1,000. Claiming that the Royal Bank of Scotland were at fault in not transferring money into the relevant account, Mr Wiltshire demanded they should compensate him. They wouldn't. And nor would the Jockey Club compensate Jonathan Sobarusa who was deprived of £8,000 winnings when a Beverley race in 1991 was off a minute early and therefore voided.

When a Wiltshire Vicar handed out tenners to his parishioners in December 1993 to help raise cash for the church restoration fund one anonymous lady used the cash to place her first ever bet on a horse race – and won £35 which she handed over to the Rev Colin Fox who said, 'She had to get her son to put the money on because she didn't know what to do.'

Fred Winter won **ninety** races and ammassed £145,915
of prize money in becoming top jump trainer
for the seventh of eight occasions in 1977-78.

'Red hot horse race favourites are exploding before they reach the winning post, claimed a story in the *Sunday Sport* of 9 January, 1994. 'The thoroughbred steeds build up so much heat that their bodies expand with gases and burst open, spattering spectators in a shower of blood and guts.' Allegedly referring to race meetings in the Middle East, the exclusive purported to be written by Rob Gelding.

The gambler at York was convinced that Grey Shot had beaten Saleel in a photo-finish outcome to a race in August 1995. So convinced that he wagered £31,000 with bookie Victor Chandler, to win £2,800. Saleel got the verdict by a short head.

'I love a bet. I'd be mad not to in my position, because I have such a close affinity with my horses. On the occasions we go for a gamble I tell my owners I'll get it right eight times out of ten.' Gay Kelleway whose BMW was paid for by one successful coup.

The Queen ordered a stewards' enquiry after a couple married in the Royal Box at Epsom racecourse. Mark and Kim Daly were the first couple to wed there, in September 1995, but when the Queen found out she made it clear that she was not amused and Epsom had to agree to call the Royal Box the Marriage Room for future nuptials. A Palace spokesman was quoted as saying: 'We have no objections to the marriage, but we are trying to avoid the exploitation of the Royal Box.' Cheltenham became the first course to be licensed to stage marriages, in August 1995.

In 1825 a horse called Lottery – father of the horse of the same name who would, in 1839, win the first Grand National – was so highly rated that when he was entered for the Borough Members' Plate, worth 70 sovereigns, at Preston, no other owner would enter a horse against him. In desperation, to ensure that a competitive race would take place, it was decided – for perhaps the only occasion on record – to offer Lottery's owner 20 guineas to withdraw from the race.

At the age of **ninety-two**, owner Jim Joel saw his Maori Venture win the 1987 Grand National.

THE BROADCAST BRIGADE

'. . . whose relaxed charm is belied by his staring eyes. He looks like a missionary, the kind of chap who might show up on your doorstep to persuade you to join the Temple of Temperate Tipsters. When McGrath recommends a horse, you *believe*.' Do you think Andrew Baker of the *Independent on Sunday* is calling Jim McGrath a cult?

'Racing's most incisive analyst? – John Francome. The worst? That awful refugee from Dr Who's Tardis, John McCririck.' *Daily Express* TV critic Frank Malley.

'His fashion statement is unsubtle. It says: bollocks.' The *Guardian*'s Pass Notes column on John McCririck.

'A man who has only to open his mouth to confuse me.' More Big Mac praise from *The Times*' Matthew Bond.

Wealthy film producer Cornelius Vanderbilt 'Sonny' Whitney, whose Phalanx and Counterpoint won the Belmont Stakes in 1947 and 51, died aged **ninety-three** in 1992.

'It will contribute to his weight problem and increase his risk of heart disease and some cancers.' Adrienne Cullum of the British Nutrition Foundation, analysing John McCririck's eating habits as revealed in the *Sunday Mirror Magazine* in March 1995 in which he said: 'I sort of graze off the chuck wagon at the races. Sausage and bacon rolls. Fried bread.'

'I always felt his great strength was behind the camera . . . and whether it's in the interest of coverage to have him in vision is clearly for others to decide.' Implied dig at McCririck from fellow Harrow School old-boy Julian Wilson, himself, of course, a walking charisma-fest in front of the cameras.

'If terrestrial television comes to negotiate for the Derby knowing we cannot have Sky or a channel like them as a potential bidder our negotiating ability is decreased. We are at a disadvantage against all those sporting events which are not listed by the Act. That cannot be in the interests of horse racing.' David Hillyard, managing director of the Race Horse Trust, apparently arguing in the *Daily Mail* against the Derby being guaranteed live coverage by terrestrial TV.

The second of Josh Gifford's four jump jockey titles was landed with **ninety-four** victories in 1963-64.

'I don't suppose Paul Holley would be too enamoured of the thought of Richard Dunwoody breathing up his bottom as they go to the last.' Thought-provoking pre-race comment on BBC2 by Peter Scudamore covering a meeting at Ascot in November 1995.

'If someone else is paying I normally charge first and go tourist.' Champion jockey (Greatest Jockey according to McCririck) turned TV celeb, John Francome, who might find his expense claims are scrutinized slightly more closely following this 1995 admission.

'The first single sport channel . . . rightly puts gambling on horses and dogs in a quarter where the only room it takes up is that of its devotees.' *Daily Mail* TV critic Neil Wilson who, one might suspect, is not the greatest racing fan around, discussing the Racing Channel in an article which described his own paper's racing coverage as 'a free service to the bookmaking industry' – as if the TV pages weren't a free service to the television industry.

The Queen Mum, aged **ninety-five**, celebrated a record fifth win in Sandown's Horse & Hound Gold Cup with Norman Conqueror in 1996.

'Any horse looks fast running past trees.' Wonderful put-down from *Coronation Street*'s Vera Duckworth to TV husband Jack, dreaming of glory with the hurdler he and his drinking cronies from the Rovers Return had just bought, Betty's Hot Shot, in April 1996.

'My Latin teacher at prep school caught me reading the *Sporting Life* at the back of the class and, instead of bollocking me, asked me what he should back. He won 30-odd quid (a lot of money in 1969) and taught me a lot about man management.' *Radio 5 Live* and *Rugby Special*'s John Inverdale.

'She was the most beautiful girl I'd ever seen in my life. I was very busy so I sent my floor manager over to her with a note.' Romantic, or what? Derek Thompson recalls the first time he met his wife Julie.

'Pathologically non-controversial.' *Racing Post* columnist Paul Haigh on Jimmy Lindley.

Quest for Fame won in California in 1992, thus becoming the first Derby winner for **ninety-seven** years to win as a five year old.

'Frankie Dettori should ride at least something to victory at Carlisle this afternoon.' *Radio 5 Live*'s Cornelius Lysaght with a somewhat desperate-sounding tip for listeners on 30 May 1996. And he didn't!

'Could be even better with another summer's grass on his back.' Now, that *would* be worth seeing – Mark Pitman, on the Racing Channel, tipping his stable's Nahthen Lad as a potential 1997 Cheltenham Gold Cup winner but perhaps with that sort of preparation he'd still be a bit green!

'What I do remember is David Coleman interviewing me and me having the strangest feeling that I was looking down on myself, watching the whole conversation.' Jenny Pitman revealing an 'out of body' experience after Corbiere won the 1983 Grand National.

Earlie Fires, 42, became the first jockey in the **ninety-eight** year history of the course to ride 6 winners from 6 riders at Hawthorne, USA in June 1989.

ODD OFFICIALDOM

'Many races are lost because of bad starts, jockeys falling off horses before the start, covering unnecessary ground, dropping the whip, intentional obstruction etc.' And you thought we had problems! Malaya's Perak Turf Club Chairman, the snappily named Tan Sri Dato Seri V Jeyaratnam, informs *Straits Times* readers of the problems facing their sport in May 1996.

'Get it right and nobody remembers; get it wrong and nobody forgets.' Retiring (after 44 years) Senior Judge to the Jockey Club, Michael Hancock, who once took thirty minutes to sort out a result at Newbury – an event immediately dubbed Hancock's Half Hour.

'If I wanted to dope an animal and wanted to be certain of achieving the desired effect, I would dope to stop it, not to enhance its performance.' Neville Dunnett, former head of Horseracing Forensic Laboratory.

Ninety-nine winners gave Tim Moloney the jump jockey championship in season 1951-52.

'If a new drug is found in Ireland in the morning, we and France will know about that drug by the afternoon.' Confident (let's hope with good reason) sounding Professor Bob Smith, retiring chairman of the European Horserace Scientific Liaison committee, in April 1996.

'The first three years of the BHB (British Horseracing Board) have been almost totally squandered. We need a financial plan and full-time BHB directors with commercial backgrounds who know what they're doing, not just people who are good at parties and overseas jaunts.' Now come on, Guy Harwood, don't beat about the bush – tell us what you really think of the BHB!

'If you must pull a horse, which I don't recommend, you should keep your elbows moving to make it look as though you're trying.' Brigadier Roscoe Harvey, senior stewards secretary, to an anonymous jockey he suspected of not trying hard enough during a race.

'As our racehorses are as upper class as the Jockey Club, perhaps they enjoy a good thrashing now and then.' *Observer* correspondent, Peter Moverley, of Bristol, enters the whip debate.

Banned for a day after 'pushing and kicking' another jockey during the 1996 Calcutta Derby, in which he was second, jockey Kieran Fallon was also fined **one hundred** pounds.

'I'm more amazed that the stewards were such buffoons as to ban the first three jockeys. After a magnificent finish like that, the riders deserve praise not punishment.' Claud Duval in the *Sun,* following the suspension for whip abuse of the first three jockeys home in the 1996 2,000 Guineas, which led several racing writers to point out that many jockeys were receiving more stringent penalties for trying too hard than those meted out to other jockeys for not trying hard enough.

'It always seems quite ironic that those who complain most are also those who are the most successful in handicaps.' Senior handicapper Geoffrey Gibbs in December 1995, discussing 'whingeing' trainers who complain about weight allotted to their charges.

'You don't know who everyone is and I even tried to apprehend the trainer's wife twice . . . But aside from dabbing red paint on everyone entitled to be there, it's difficult to know exactly what we can do.' Cheltenham's Edward Gillespie on the difficulties of keeping unauthorized people out of the winners' enclosure.

John Francome was champion jump jockey for the last time in 1984-85 with **one hundred and one** winners.

'Furthermore, the stewards cautioned Miss Crowley for the way she departed from the stewards' room.' Report of the Navan Stewards after Miss F M Crawley – clearly a spirited lass – was suspended for four days for careless riding in May 1996.

'It is very important racing should go on being fun – because it is nothing otherwise.' Peregrine Andrew Morny Cavendish (better known as Stoker) Hartington, stepping down from a career as senior steward of the Jockey Club and first chairman of the BHB, in May 1996. But why do so many officials only decide that life should be fun when they are no longer in a position to help make it so?

'The insane, anachronistic arrogance of the racing toffs, who so blithely dare to treat a 53-year-old great like Mr Carson like a new boy at prep school.' Perhaps Matthew Norman of the *Evening Standard* didn't agree with the five-day ban Willie Carson received in May 1996 for wearing the wrong crash helmet. It was, though, overturned on appeal.

'The pity of it was that the Jockey Club didn't explain what it was doing, and people assumed it wasn't doing anything.' Lord Hartington, on retiring in May 1996, having been chairman of the BHB and senior steward of the Jockey Club.

'We are, however, now living under a racing regime that gives seven days for throwing a race away and sometimes more than that for trying too hard to win.' *Racing Post*'s Paul Haigh, May 1996.

'If only all our legislators had their priorities as well sorted out as the estimable Mr Evans. All things considered I see him as a future Prime Minister.' *Sunday Express*'s Colonel Pinstripe, revealing that Ribble Valley Tory MP Nigel Evans had listed three days racing at the Cheltenham Festival on his Register of Members' Interests.

'My late mother would often hang my pyjamas on a washing line in winter and, depending on their stiffness the following morning, she could deliver a long-range weather forecast covering several days. I commend this to Mr Gillespie, especially if he takes the additional step of staying inside the pyjamas himself.' *Independent on Sunday*'s Stan Hey with advice for acting Clerk of the Course at Cheltenham,

Edward Gillespie. His decision not to inspect overnight despite a heavy frost, and subsequent bullish announcements about the prospects, before calling off the card at short notice 'led around 10,000 racegoers and scores of trainers and horses to arrive, only to find that Mr Gillespie had been wildly optimistic.'

'The Derby used to be the close-the-factory day out for Londoners. But there isn't a working class any more. They're all driving off to garden centres instead.' Edward Gillespie of Epsom on why the Blue Riband of the turf no longer commands the crowds of yore.

'Unable to make up their minds, the stewards requested the jockeys concerned to toss a coin to decide the result.' Probably a far better system than the traditional stewards' enquiry, reported from a late 19th-century meeting in Gloucestershire by racing historian Brian Lee.

Elnathan Flatman was the first flat jockey to break the century barrier, riding **one hundred and four** winners in 1848.

John Francome landed his third jump jockey title with
one hundred and five winners in 1980-81.

 **NAGNOTES**

'Secretariat is only human.' Steve Pinkus, connection of the US superstar horse.

'Like so many who have been retired he began to show that he actually enjoyed being in training after being taken out of it.' Toby Balding on champion hurdler Morley Street who was retired only to be brought back.

'This one's been gelded and should have a squeak.' Indeed. Simon Holt's *Morning Line* comment on a fancied runner.

'She is a very, very good mare and very beautiful too – big ears, big head and a big bum.' Beauty's in the eye of the beholder, of course. One wonders what Nicky Henderson's favourite ladies look like – something like Newbury winner Conquering Hero, perhaps.

Charlie Elliott's one outright flat jockey title was secured courtesy of **one hundred and six** winners in 1924.

'She's such a vain lady and she relaxes when she sees herself in the mirror.' Michael Stoute on filly Pure Grain, whose box came equipped with vanity mirror. Owner Coral Pritchard Gordon commented that it helped keep the filly calm: 'She thinks she can see a friend.'

'A complete loony who would be in a padded cell wearing a straitjacket were he human.' Comment on Assacombe – one not, perhaps, to trust with the family fortunes – with form figures of UFPPPFF, in 1995 Hunter Chasers and Point To Pointers.

'I don't smoke, but my horse does.' Owner Allen Paulson – who once described his Arazi as 'not just the best horse I have ever owned – the best horse anyone has ever owned' – on his brilliant Cigar, who had just won the $3 million 1995 Breeders' Cup Classic. The horse went on to contest the inaugural Dubai World Cup, prior to which jockey Jerry Bailey opined that 'only Mother Nature' could intervene to prevent victory while former member of the Cigar camp, New Yorker Tom Albertrani, who had defected to rival Godolphin set-up told his new connections: 'If you really want to beat Cigar, there's only one way to do it. Close your eyes and keep dreaming.' The optimism was well-founded as one of the most thrilling of races resulted in an awesome triumph for Cigar, who was dubbed The Best Horse In The World.

One of the greatest nineteenth century racehorses, Ormonde, ridden by Fred Archer, was the 4/9 winner of the 1886 Derby, the **one hundred and seven**th running.

'Even if he were tied to the grandstand he'd still beat this field,' said owner Ernie Paragallo of the 1996 Kentucky Derby favourite Unbridled's Song – taking a leaf out of the Cigar book. Small problem – the horse ran as though it *were* attached to the grandstand and was unplaced.

'Rather a sweet little horse. But unfortunately no bloody good.' Trainer John Dunlop on the most expensive yearling of all, $10.2m (£6.6m) Snaafi Dancer, who never ran a single race.

'If I had known what that horse would do to me today, I would have let the bugger die.' Dick Francis after the 1949 Grand National in which Russian Hero, whom Francis had saved from potentially fatal colic, won at 66/1 – beating Francis on Roimond into second place.

'Lucky they didn't use my real name. Can you imagine rooting for a horse called Sheldon Greenfield?' US comic Shecky Greene after having a horse named after him.

Dick (Frederick Bilbo) Rees was the first jump jockey to crack the century barrier when he rode **one hundred and eight** winners from just 348 mounts in 1924.

'This colt is a champion. He could gallop down the side of a house.' Dick Hern on triple-crown-winning Nashwan.

'After Silver Wedge won the Queen's Vase at Royal Ascot we were asked to come back the next day to collect the trophy from the weighing room. . . We duly returned the following day – and officials prevented us from entering the weighing room.' Owner Bill Robins.

'He's still got his balls. You'd make sure you cleared the hurdles if your tackle was still there.' Owner of champion hurdler Alderbrook, Ernie Pick, explaining his horse's excellent jumping style in March 1995.

'Equipped with high-tech blinkers, his ears stuffed with cotton wool, and covered by a bright yellow hood.' It must have been a wonder Rambrino knew where he was and where he was headed as he won the 1996 Cockspur Cup at the Garrison Savannah in Barbados, for owner Robert Sangster. The horse, who had a 'rogue's reputation', was trained by Sean Hall, son of West Indies fast bowler, Wes, at 10/1.

Henry Cecil trained **one hundred and nine** winners for prize money of £382,301 in becoming leading trainer of 1978, his second title.

'The thoroughbred is a delicate animal, women's tender feelings may help a horse.' Top Japanese jockey Yutaka Take on the debut of women jockeys in Japanese racing, in March 1996.

'If King's Theatre wins a Derby I will emigrate to Rwanda.' Bold assertion by breeding expert, James Underwood, editor of the *European Racing & Breeding Digest* in 1994, backing up his opinion of the staying powers of the highly rated colt. The air tickets were never needed, but it was a close run thing, with King's Theatre runner-up in the 1994 Derby.

'On balance the sporting horse enjoys a better life than it would in the wild, where the injured, aged or enfeebled animal can only hope to peg out before the circling wolves or vultures move in for lunch.' Geoffrey Phillips of the *Evening Standard*.

'The horse is a creature of flight, not fright. Whoever heard of Mother Nature using the whip on the fleetest mustang as it leads the pack?' Racing writer Roy David of the *Manchester Evening News* with a contribution to the whip debate.

'I started running her over a mile and a quarter and a mile and a half – in those races she would have to breathe or she would drop dead!' Trainer Roland O'Sullivan on how he finally put paid to filly La Petite Fusee's habit of trying to complete her sprint races by running from start to finish without taking a breath. It worked – and she won at Lingfield over six furlongs when dropped back in distance.

'It all started when he began kicking his water buckets out of the stable. So I bought him a football and now we both play – he's even learnt to trap it under his foot.' Stable lad George Wake in 1994 on his Tom Jones-trained charge, Alami.

'He pees to his own line and length.' Trainer Tony Hide on the bizarre affliction suffered by his beautifully named 1994 two-year-old, Backward Point, born with his genitals back to front.

Relatives and admirers attended a celebration in October 1992 at the London pub named after a flamboyant racecourse tipster, Prince Monolulu, on what would have been his **one hundred and eleven**th birthday.

1891 saw odds on favourite, Common, win the
one hundred and twelfth Derby ridden by George Barrett.

NATIONAL NATTER

'When my horses go out to run in the National they are a bit like aircraft going to war. I hope they come back in one piece with no war wounds or bullet holes.' Dual National winner, Jenny Pitman.

'I am simply not interested in the race. It has never done anything for me. It is too full of emotion; so exciting beforehand and too upsetting afterwards.' Jockey Graham McCourt.

'Remember, it was the height of the Cold War, and apparently there were some Soviet bigwigs in the crowd. I was told that they had planted an electric wire just under the turf by the water jump.' Queen Mum's jockey turned best-selling novelist, Dick Francis, revealing one of the least likely explanations as to why his mount Devon Loch collapsed when clear on the run-in of the 1956 Grand National. Amongst the other reasons put forward have been: crowd noise;

Sir Hugo was a shock winner of the **one hundred and thirteen**th Derby, run in 1892, at odds of 40/1, beating hot favourite, La Fleche.

broken blood vessel; attack of cramp; muscular seizure; and, according to the *People* newspaper in 1991: 'Devon Loch's back legs almost certainly gave way because of the most natural reason in the world. It let rip with a good old-fashioned fart.'

'Those who would have us believe that the horses are made to suffer for our enjoyment are barking up the wrong tree. Watch the face of the horse that comes in today. It will be wreathed in smiles.' Slightly surreal *Daily Telegraph* Leader Column comment on the morning of the 1996 National.

'I was left sitting on top of the fence with nearly 40 other runners liable to land on me at any moment. I scrambled down and ran for my life. Next day there was a picture in the paper of me sprinting flat out, and I thought I'd been rumbled. But the caption said: "Pile up at the 23rd – Stan Mellor runs after his mount."' Stan Mellor on the 1967 fiasco in which he rode The Fossa whose fall began the mass pile-up which resulted in 100/1 no-hoper Foinavon's victory.

Big Racket clocked a record 43.26mph in a two furlong race in Mexico City in Feburary 1995, carrying **one hundred and fourteen** pounds.

'The Grand National is a great spectacle, a great institution but, in spite of all the hype, it isn't, in fact, a very good race.' Unless you train the winner, that is, perhaps. Trainer David Elsworth reported by Hugh McIlvanney in 1990.

'There are disappointing signs that the magic of the National may have peaked and could even be on the wane.' With TV audiences for the National in decline by millions, Richard Evans, racing correspondent of *The Times*, raises an issue which must be confronted.

'The World's greatest steeplechase exists because of Aintree, the sponsors, the owners of the horses and the bravery of the jockeys who ride them. How dare anyone restrict the amount of money they can raise for their efforts.' *Independent on Sunday* sports writer Peter Corrigan arguing in favour of the National – and Derby – being able to sell themselves to satellite TV if they choose. At which point, one might argue, their TV audience will diminish even further.

Danny Maher's second jockey title was gained in 1913 with **one hundred and fifteen** winners.

'A woman jockey could jump the race backwards and still survive. In the old days it was tough, but now they've become powder-puff fences.' National winning trainer Josh Gifford.

'The very title of the race gives the game away: the Grand National is part of the way the British see themselves; the ghosts of Balaclava and Inkerman lurk in its history.' The always perceptive Simon Barnes.

Michael Stoute-trained runners landed **one hundred and sixteen** victories and £1,360,708 prize money as he became 1989 champion.

ANIMAL MAGIC AT THE RACES

RABBITS ate through a cable at the rear of Royal Ascot's giant TV screen in front of the grandstand in 1995 – blanking out the screen.

A BULLOCK had to be removed from the track at Beverley before the runners for the 2.15 in May 1989 could be sent on their way.

A FLOCK OF SHEEP delayed the start of the 1988 Ulster Derby at Down Royal.

A GREYHOUND finished fourth in the 2.15 Lingfield in December 1986 having strayed on to the course.

Jonjo O'Neill's second and final jump jockey championship winning total was **one hundred and seventeen** in 1979-80.

A SEAGULL was blamed for the 1992 death of Aussie jockey Neil Barker, flying in front of his mount, Father Time, at Randwick.

A TROOP OF BABOONS had to be moved on before racing could resume at Nairobi in 1992.

SNAKES spooked the runners at Adelaide in 1928 and had to be killed before the race took place.

A GROUP OF BLACK SWANS was the unexpected obstacle which faced Jamie Bruin on Atlantalady as they led the race at River Downs, Kentucky in 1995. They leapt the birds and went on to win.

A FOX sunning himself at Gulfstream Park in 1991 caused Julie Krone and Quilma to jump and swerve, costing them the race in which they finished second.

A COW sacrifice was demanded by superstitious jockeys at Accra, Ghana, in 1966 after accidents had plagued a bend on the course. The riders believed that a sacrifice would placate the gods. Officials refused and banned the jockeys.

A LABRADOR ran across the open ditch at Chepstow during the 1936 Welsh National, causing four horses to fall.

A BLACK COCKER SPANIEL interfered with Jimmy Lindley and Indiana during the 1964 St Leger, but they took evasive action and won.

RHINOS on the track interrupted racing at Racecourse Road, Kenya, in 1903.

A DOG raced on to the track at Hamilton in May 1996 and tried to bite two of the runners in the East Kilbride Handicap. Said Kevin Darley, riding in the race, 'I saw Dean's [McKeown's] horse jump over the dog as it raced back off the track.'

In winning his three Grand Nationals, Red Rum beat **one hundred and nineteen** opponents.

TRAINER CHAT

'I was too busy dancing around to let it sink in, and want to win it again so that I can sit back and appreciate it.' Peter Chapple-Hyam on winning the Derby with Dr Devious – greedy or what?

'A good helping of beef never did anyone any harm.' Bullish if debatable sentiment from trainer Ken Oliver during the height of the 1996 Mad Cow scare. Oliver announced that he would be buying horses to race bearing pro-beef eating slogans. Of course, Ken could afford to take this attitude – he didn't have that much to lose if he turned out to be wrong – after all he was already 82 years old at the time.

'I'd help out the Troggs when their regular drummer was sick or went on holiday.' Trainer Richard Hannon finally admitted to his long-rumoured secret past life as a rock 'n' roll animal in a *Daily Telegraph* interview in April 1996, which proved conclusively that he couldn't control himself!

John Francome (who stopped riding when his opponent was injured) and Peter Scudamore shared the jump jockey title with **one hundred and twenty** winners apiece.

'I may have been a bit surprised when we were beaten, but one report even had me down as "ashen-faced". Ashen-faced! I ask you. What a load of bollocks.' Major fit of pique from Dick Hern on his reported reaction to the first-time-out defeat of his 1996 2,000 Guineas favourite (finished fourth in the Classic), Alhaarth.

'Some horses will work like a dream in the morning, but come the afternoon you can't find them with a search warrant.' A plea for morning racing, perhaps, from John Gosden.

'You don't have to cheat to win races. You know when a horse has come right and if you've got a horse you can win with, you want it to win. It's your calling card.' Shrewd winner of handicaps and scourge of the bookies, Reg Akehurst.

'They are born with the talent they have got. What we are trying to do is to let them show it and not mess them up.' US trainer Charlie 'Bald Eagle' Whittingham. In fact Whittingham is so dedicated to his horses that when one of his best ones kicked him hard his first thought was to check that the horse had not injured itself in the process.

Fred Winter set a then record total of **one hundred and twenty-one** winners in taking the 1952-53 jump jockey title.

'An Eton and Sandhurst man who had a leg blown off in Korea, he is said to travel with three artificial legs; one for shooting, one for riding and one for dancing.' Robin Oakley on trainer Fergie Sutherland – clearly the man to have on your side when you're waiting for the final leg of your bet to come up.

'Any bloody fool can win with a two-year-old – it takes a bit of management to win 16 handicaps with a horse.' The aforementioned Fergie Sutherland, who achieved just that feat with his Fox King.

'You could never meet anyone more obnoxious than those little flat jockeys, could you?' Trainer Noel T Chance's contribution to good working relationships between handlers and riders as reported by the *Sporting Life* in February 1996.

'I got a job with a man, Vic Thompson, who made Hitler look like a choirboy.' Noel T Chance, who could be accused of modelling his own style on the infamous dictator, on his first job in Australia.

Jockey turned trainer and MBE, Josh Gifford, rode **one hundred and twenty-two** winners in his best season over jumps, 1966-67.

'There are plenty of people who train horses who think they are saving the world rather than preparing beasts to run round a field.' Richard Edmondson putting the skills of trainers into perspective in the *Independent*.

'We should remember when we are rollocking jockeys that it is a job where the ambulance follows you when you are working.' Trainer Bill O'Gorman.

'Nobody ever commits suicide if he has a young horse.' Octogenarian US trainer Charlie Whittingham.

'You can criticize a trainer's wife, but never his horses.' Geoff Lester of the *Sporting Life* on Trainer Mark Wilkinson's resentment at criticism of his No Fiddling.

'Trainers . . . could be licensed according to a grading system. Grade One trainers could have runners at Grade One and Grade Two tracks, but not Grade Three. Grade Two trainers could operate at all levels, but Grade Three stables would not be allowed to compete in Grade One.' Radical proposal put forward in January 1996 by bookmaker Victor Chandler.

Samuel Kenyon won the flat jockey championship just once, with **one hundred and twenty-three** winners in 1866.

'If size meant anything, a cow would beat a rabbit.' Herb Stevens, US handler, on being told one of his horses was too small to win the Kentucky Derby.

'Personally, I have enough trouble trying to account to myself and my owner for a disappointing run without having to manufacture a spurious malady to satisfy some hobgoblin in Portman Square.' Tom Jones', not the Welsh superstar, opinion of the Jockey Club requirement to offer an explanation for poor performances, introduced early in 1996.

'I'm probably too much of a horse-lover to be really successful.' Trainer Terry Casey speaking a month or two before his Rough Quest won the 1996 Grand National.

'Buying horses in Ireland is like playing poker. When you see the real thing it is similar to picking up a cracking hand of cards. You mustn't let on.' Jenny Pitman – no doubt a mean card player.

Aussie mare, Ouroene, was beaten in **one hundred and twenty-four** consecutive races between 1976 and 1983.

'It's never easy for a young trainer, and I don't give a damn about how much money he's got. It could be that the more money he's got the less chance he has of succeeding because he's not hungry.' Peter Easterby.

'I went to take a throw-in and noticed the lad was holding up two fingers. I wasn't sure if it meant I was playing like a prat or Jamesmead had finished second.' Mick Channon recalling the days when he was combining his two loves, football and racing – and he was out on the pitch while his horse contested a race.

'When I go to meet my maker at the Pearly Gates he'll ask what I did in life and when I answer "racehorse trainer, sir" he'll say "A what, for Pete's sake? I've got the likes of Mother Teresa in here."' Sir Mark Prescott, playing down his role in life in a *Racing Post* interview during which he highlighted the nature of his calling thus: 'I'm a firm believer that training is what doesn't go wrong as opposed to what goes right. A happy trainer is a bad trainer; the worse the trainer the happier he is because he hasn't noticed what's going on.' And if that wasn't scathing enough,he noted: 'It must be remembered that all horses are trying to kill themselves, and all lads are aiding and abetting them.'

Ron Barry clocked up **one hundred and twenty-five** winners to land the first of two jump jockey titles in 1972-73.

'Before vaccinations became compulsory, horses never got flu twice.' Peter Easterby, sceptical of the value of preventative medicine.

'Britain is supposed to be the cradle of racing, yet we have a programme which favours bad horses – it's all very cynical.' Bill O'Gorman.

'He may be a late starter, but he's an early finisher.' US trainer Bob Ussery on his horse Reflected Glory.

'He asked if I'd always be available. When I said yes, he pressed half a crown into my hand and said, "Right, here's your retainer, then."' Now-retired jockey Brian Rouse recalling his acceptance by legendary trainer Ryan Price.

'You realize that God doesn't actually mind whether you win or not. You look at the children of the world who are deprived, abused, ill-treated, starving – you get much more realistic.' Henry Cecil, putting the importance of racing into perspective.

6-year-old, Zany Tactics, carried **one hundred and twenty-six** pounds in setting a world record time of 1m.06.8s for six furlongs at Turf Paradise, USA, in March 1987.

'If you start a restaurant and at the end of the year you have only three customers a day, you go bust. A trainer who has only three winners a year keeps going, and his lack of success is always someone else's fault.' French trainer Jean-Claude Rouget.

'Just how much of the actual training one person is able to do with 100 or more is open to question.' Peter Walwyn advocating a rule restricting strings to a maximum of 100.

'You cannot put a saddle on a pedigree.' John Gosden.

'When I lost my licence to ride I started a few sidelines, trading in just about anything: vodka, chicken legs, oil, gas, diamonds, works of art and even a submarine . . . and then I decided to have a go at training.' Charlie Mann.

'You should treat every horse as a good horse until you know it isn't. The minute you know that, you should get rid of it, yesterday if possible.' David Gandolfo.

Spearmint won the 1906 Derby, the **one hundred and twenty-seven**th, at 6/1, ridden by Danny Maher.

'If they're not nice rides, one tries to send them to heaven, quite honestly. An unrideable racehorse is a very difficult animal to accommodate.' Toby Balding on the fate of ex-racehorses.

'I wouldn't want to do an Eric Cantona. Not go over the top. No, I'd have given that fan a bad horse. It would have cost him money and it would have given him grief.' Mick Channon offers a novel alternative punishment for Cantona's tormentor.

'In this business there's always something coming along to give you another kick up the arse.' Jim Old, speaking well before the 1996 incident in which his stables burned down.

'Surely a horse is either off or not off – just the same as a girl can't be a little bit pregnant.' Colin Tinkler on varying non-trying punishments and penalties.

'We are turning racing into a circus and have lost our way somewhere if we believe that clowns and dancing girls are necessary to attract people to the racecourse.' Reg Akehurst on Sunday racing.

One hundred and twenty-eight Henry Cecil-trained winners picked up prize money of £683,971 as he became 1979 champion.

'I think they handicap trainers as much as horses and, under the current system, it doesn't pay to be straight.' Trainer Reg Akehurst, unhappy at the raising in the weights of one of his charges in November 1995.

'You will only retire when I tell you to.' Newmarket handler Tom Jones recalling the words of owner Sheikh Hamdan when he (Jones) was erroneously reported to be on the verge of packing it all in.

'I buy racehorses cheap, not cheap racehorses.' Welsh trainer Ron Boss.

'The stewards have to be guided by the jockeys, and they couldn't wait to get home. What exactly are they rushing home for? *Neighbours?*' Irate Richard Rowe after a blizzard caused Plumpton to be abandoned in December 1995.

'It's like looking at a lady. She should be pretty with a fine head and good, large, honest eye, nothing small or mean about it. Her conformation must be exceptional and of course she should move well.' Vincent O'Brien on the attributes of an outstanding mare.

'People describe training as an art and a science, but a lot of it is just bloody common sense.' Les Eyre.

'If you are in racing, you are in it. There is racing and only racing. It's a world largely insulated from the real world.' Former US trainer Mark Reid, who quit in 1992.

'We use the car to do a job with – we use the horse to do a job with.' Trainer Dai Burchell on TV documentary *They Shoot Horses, Don't They*, on the fate of ex-racehorses, shown in October, 1995, in which Bill O'Gorman revealed his attitude to the animals in his charge: 'I wouldn't say I like them. I'd say I respect them because I get my living from them.'

'We're as fond of our horses as most people are of their wives.' Charlie Brooks on the eve of the 1995 Grand National at which time he had no wife.

'As far as I can see, unless you're dishonest,it's impossible to make any money if you're a National Hunt trainer.' Charlie Brooks who, in the same Sunday

---

7-year-old, Il Tempo, set a world record time of 3m.16.75s for two miles in New Zealand in 1970, carrying **one hundred and thirty** pounds.

paper interview, confessed: 'I hate going racing. I hate all the small talk, all the nervous chit-chat. I'd rather watch it on television.'

'Our methods are out of touch on an international scale. We stand back and admire bloodstock, find reasons not to run animals bred to race. European owners and trainers lucky enough to have a good horse go to great lengths to avoid somebody else's animal of equal class, fearing defeat . . . In the United States there is little dishonour in losing and great determination to win next time.' Swingeing attack by *Evening Standard* racing writer Christopher Poole.

'In general I've always thought British trainers are the worst in the world. Change comes so slowly . . . As a group our trainers are the least competent in the business.' So that's John McCririck's chances of being elected to run the National Trainers' Federation scuppered.

'What we do is very inexact, and horses can make an arse of you.' Michael Stoute.

John Francome's largest haul of winners in seven title winning seasons was **one hundred and thirty-one** in 1983-84.

'I am a bit of a freak in the racing world – a man for all seasons, ten years ahead of my time.' Plain speaking former jockey Paul 'Martin Peters' Kelleway who also declared in a May 1996 interview: 'Ability does not get you a glass of water in racing. It is not what you know but who you know.'

'He has called me a prat so often I was beginning to think it was my second name.' Trainer Charlie Moore on his relationship with volatile owner Ken Higson.

'If you don't have friends, winning the Kentucky Derby doesn't mean much, anyway.' William Young, owner of the 1996 Derby winner, Grindstone, in response to questioners asking why he'd kept his horses with Wayne Lukas when he went through a lean spell.

'I could name licensed trainers in this country who could not manage to perform even the most basic task of putting a bridle on a horse, and there are a few as well who would have no idea of how to make an entry.' Irish racing pundit Ted Walsh.

Willie Carson gained his first jockey championship with **one hundred and thirty-two** winners in 1972.

'I'm old enough to be his grandfather anyway and I thought it might be a bit selfish to carry on. It would be rather embarrassing having your father coming to school in a wheelchair, don't you think?' Then (May 1996) 53-year-old Henry Cecil on how concern for his two-year-old son, Jake, persuaded him to give up the dreaded weed: 'I went from cigars to Players to Silk Cut, about forty or fifty a day, to nothing.'

'The three most important elements in a horse are brain, heart and lungs – in that order – and you can't see any of them.' Forties and fifties US trainer Benjamin Allyn Jones who, when asked why he put the brain first, replied: 'Because you can't train a stupid horse.'

'They've got nothing to protect, so what's the use of covering their ....ing heads.' Trainer Towser Gosden (father of John) quoted in 1956 when skullcaps were made compulsory for jockeys.

'I go out to win – never to be second – and I would rather win a seller than be second in the Gold Cup.' Martin Pipe who has already won well over 2,000

races and wants more – Arthur Stephenson's record 2,632 is in his sights and he says, 'maybe we could yet get to 3000'.

'I started with hasbeens that never were and wannabees that never would be.' Trainer and former jockey Norman Babbage.

'He would fancy his chances if he were saddling a pregnant rhinoceros.' *Observer* writer Nick Green on Paul Kelleway.

'Win if you can but under no circumstances do I want him to have a hard race.' The remarkable riding instructions issued by trainer Arthur Budgett to jockey Eddie Hide, before he went out to partner Morston in the Derby – which, of course, he won – in 1973. Budgett dismissed criticism of the Blue Riband with the comment: 'The Derby means everything. There'll never be a time when it doesn't.'

Carrying **one hundred and thirty-four** pounds, 4-year-old Dr Fager
set a world record 1m 32.2s for one mile at
Arlington Park, USA in August 1968.

The 1992 3-year-old classifications saw Irish Derby winner, St Jovite, controversially rated on **one hundred and thirty-five** – 10lb above Derby winner, Dr Devious.

'Wearing lightweight wellies and making sure your moustache is aerodynamic would also help.' Martin Pipe responding in September 1995 to a spoof application by novice rider Tim Doxsey to replace Richard Dunwoody as stable jockey.

'Horses are just like women. You've got to spank them a little.' Top US Quarter Horse trainer, Johnnie C Goodman, 55, a man who has clearly never met Jenny Pitman and who boasts: 'I've got 13 children out of 12 different women, mostly in Texas. And they all love me.' Possibly because he has saddled the winner of the top Quarter Horse race, the All American Futurity, a 440-yard sprint with a first prize of 1 million dollars.

'British trainers try to devise ways of avoiding running their horses against animals of comparable ability. The end result: uncompetitive sport for which racegoers are asked to pay the highest admission charges in the world.' Christopher Poole, *Evening Standard.*

'Years ago I could enjoy a winner for a week, now I enjoy one for ten minutes and then I want another.' Martin Pipe. And I thought he was talking about Chinese meals!

Steve Donoghue partnered 11/10 favourite Pommern to win the 1915 Derby, the **one hundred and thirty-six**th, which was run at Newmarket.

'I have just seen hope disappear over the horizon with its backside on fire.' Peter Scudamore recalling the comment of the female trainer of a horse called Trout Angler, caught on the line when eased on the run-in by Graham Bradley some time ago.

'I am considered the scruffiest trainer in racing, so I think I am beyond help.' Do I detect an element of pride in Colin Weedon's statement?

'Everyone has been most welcoming and courteous with the exception of one certain trainer. But I must stress this one man's attitude doesn't bother me, and it doesn't matter to me because I don't allow it to spoil my enjoyment of the wonderful racing in Britain.' François Doumen on his mystery enemy, speaking in late 1994.

'I don't know why I have to wake up every morning and defend myself in these situations. I'm trying to do a job. I do it with my style and flair and I think I would be less of a person if I did it any other way.' US trainer Wayne Lukas, heavily criticized in his homeland for his methods, even though the 1995 Kentucky Derby victory of Grindstone gave him an incredible

---

Galgo Jr won a record **one hundred and thirty-seven** times during his career in Puerto Rico between 1930 and 1936.

sixth consecutive winner of a Triple Crown race. Even highly respected magazine *Sports Illustrated*'s writer William Nack observed: 'This year he entered five horses [in the Derby] a record for a trainer, which gave him more than a quarter of the field. The Derby is supposed to show who has the most horse, not the most horses.' The next week, *SI* quoted an anonymous trainer as saying: 'You never see any good four-year-olds coming out of there, do you?' nodding at the Lukas barn, 'adding weight to the ongoing criticism of Lukas – that he pushes his horses so hard an uncommon number break down.' One cannot but think that the words 'envy' and 'green' come to mind – and that Martin Pipe may have a flicker of recognition at such a reaction to success.

'Surroundings don't matter that much to a horse. Look at those athletes that are brought up in not much more than mud huts in Kenya. They come over here and wipe the floor with us.' Trainer Bryan McMahon, confessing that his yard is 'tattier than most but the horses don't know that' before sending out Jack Jennings to contest the 1996 Derby.

Gay Crusader ridden by Steve Donoghue won the
one hundred and thirty-eighth Derby in 1917, starting at 7/4.

FINAL FURLONG

The Rev John Manchester, vicar of Old Malton, North Yorkshire, began blessing local runners in spring 1996. He started with Tim Etherington's Be Brave and commented: 'I've blessed lots of pets, from ferrets to stick insects. Why not horses?'

A whole racecourse was blessed in May 1996 by 25 monks who gave Hong Kong's Happy Valley a traditional Buddhist earth blessing following a spate of accidents at the track.

Ghostly goings-on afflicted Epsom racecourse in April 1996 when course Sales Manager Marilyn Watkinson reported seeing a Lady In Black whilst working late and alone: 'She appeared to me in the 1914 building, part of the racecourse offices which used to be a hospital during the Second World War. It suddenly felt very cold. Then she appeared in the room wearing a long gown. I really was rather scared.' Other sightings date from 1992.

Daniel Maher, US champion jockey in 1898, added the British version in 1908 with **one hundred and thirty-nine** victories.

The late cartoonist Carl Giles caused a storm when asked to draw a design for the Injured Jockeys' Fund Christmas card. 'He drew a fine cartoon of a jockey in silks in hospital with a plastered leg hanging in traction,' said IJF patron Lord Oaksey. 'We thought it was funny. The jockeys thought it was funny. The public thought it was in the most appalling taste. Giles, I'm afraid, was never asked again.'

Trainer Tom Jones told the tale of old-time trainer Sid Forrell, one of whose owners demanded a straight to the point telegram of explanation following the run of a horse. The owner duly received one bearing the cryptic message: SF SF SF SF. Baffled, the owner requested an explanation when they met: 'Started, farted, slipped and fell. See you Friday, Sid Forrell.'

Jockey Lee Newton was really riding for a fall when he went for a sneaky drive whilst still banned – because the car had his name emblazoned on the side! Local police, aware of his ban, spotted the sponsored car and recognized Newton at the wheel. He claimed he was driving the car to be sold – and was sentenced to 80 hours' community service and £30 costs.

Lucky Express was the **one hundred and forty** to one winner at Hong Kong's Sha-tin in February 1993, producing a record tierce (1-2-3) dividend of HK$390,697 for HK$10.

Food fads are usually associated with humans – but horses have their little quirks, too. English-born Sally Bailie, training in the States, had one horse who was passionate about blueberry muffins, and another who would share a stablehand's hot tea. Also in the States, trainer Richard DeStasio's Bit Of Coral was partial to hamburgers (a risk of mad horse disease here, perhaps?), while Spicy Monarch was anyone's for a ham and cheese sandwich. Bobby Barbara reported a bacon and eggs loving stable inmate, while Angel Cordero had an ice-loving pony.

Marypats Secret, trained by Red Terrill, would not tolerate anyone else in the yard eating cream cheese bagels unless she had one herself.

Damien Hirst's dead sheep caused controversy in the art world – and artist Mark Wallinger achieved a similar feat in the racing world when, in March 1994, he declared that his latest work of art was a racehorse actually called A Real Work Of Art, which he purchased for 6600 guineas with the help of a consortium of collectors and dealers – and placed in training with Sir Mark Prescott.

Opinions were divided over whether a real horse could be a work of art. The *Daily Telegraph* critic Richard Dorment, though, was in no doubt: 'If art is about much more than manual dexterity, and if it is the artist's job to use every means at his disposal to make us aware of the beauty and interest to be found in the

Humorist won Epsom Derby number **one hundred and forty-two** in 1921, but was dead within days after a haemmorhage of the lungs.

world around us, then I don't see why A Real Work Of Art is not just that: a real work of art.' Sadly, the horse's form would not have been suitable for exhibition and he never won in this country, although he finally landed a race in Europe.

It was difficult to contest the artist's comment that A Real Work Of Art was 'the best and most realistic representation of what she is you'll ever find. She's a pretty good likeness of herself.'

The Jockeys Guild of America spent seven years endeavouring to launch a range of clothes and souvenirs to help raise cash for its disabled Jockeys' Fund – only to be legally blocked by Jockey International, who claimed copyright over the word jockey as they sell underwear of that name and didn't want anyone else using the word – not even jockeys.

Commented a spokesman, 'Besides underwear we produce a lot of things that are like the line that jockeys are coming out with.' Eventually the Guild had to produce goods unencumbered with the word jockey – but in an effort to get their own back sought opportunities of endorsing rivals' brands of underwear!

Winning a £22 bet on Miinnehoma in the 1994 Grand National put punter Marie Lazenby in hospital. For as the horse crossed the line she jumped for joy and

36-year-old US trainer, Rodney Rash, died in February 1996, with **one hundred and forty-three** winners to his credit.

cheered – so upsetting her pet golden retriever that it jumped up – and bit her on the left nipple. 27-year-old Marie was rushed to hospital in Middlesbrough where the doctor who treated said: 'I have to ask – it *was* a dog and not your boyfriend?'

When Manchester City chairman Francis Lee, also a racehorse trainer, was concerned over a knee ligament injury sustained by midfielder Paul Lake, he put the player on tablets he gives to his horses.

'My knee used to swell up badly after a couple of days' training, but the tablets worked wonders,' said Lake. Lee commented:'The pills are homeopathic tablets diluted from the strengths we give our horses.'

Rumours that Lake would be entered in the Grand National proved unfounded.

Fellow jockeys helped Tony Dobbin celebrate his 22nd birthday at Hexham racecourse in May 1994 – by covering his genitals with black boot polish.

Racing commentators came under fire in 1994 when an Irish politician accused them of 'deliberately insulting the Irish people'. And their offence? Mispronouncing horses with Gaelic names. Raged former Agriculture

Minister Austin Deasy: 'If it were Japanese, Czechoslovakian, Arabic, Chinese or French, they would have it perfect. But if it is Irish you get the greatest bastardization of all time.'

Weight watching is a permanent bugbear for jockeys – few though, could match the achievement of Canadian jockey Miriam 'Mini' McTague who, in 1994, shed an astounding *eighty-four pounds* to make the weight of 7st for her debut ride at Woodbine, Ontario.

Richard Dunwoody and Miinnehoma became the first racing figures featured on BT Phonecards after their 1994 Grand National triumph when a limited edition of 500 were produced. They are now colletors' items with other similarly rare examples going for over £2000 in mint condition.

Owner Robert Perez was looking forward to watching his filly Cupecoy's Joy contesting the 1982 Preakness Stakes, one of the American triple crown races. The Argentinian-born owner arrived at the Pimlico track where he had booked a table at the restaurant, only to be told that there was no record of his reservation. He stormed out of the restaurant – and promptly scratched his horse from the race.

Mornington Cannon was champion flat jockey for the sixth and final time in 1897, with **one hundred and forty-five** winners.

Chelsea Cooksey is the youngest rider ever to win a race. Mind you, she knew little about the feat – achieving it by going along for the ride when her five-month pregnant Mum, Patti Cooksey – the top US female rider before the arrival of Julie Krone – landed her last winner before taking time off to give birth to her daughter in early 1992, naming her after one of her regular rides, Chelsea's Pet.

Racecourse tic-tac man Eddie Brown's last wish was granted in July 1994 when his horse-drawn hearse passed a string of betting shops in the Preston area en route to his final resting place.

Symmetrical horses run faster than lopsided ones, concluded biologists at Liverpool University after taking detailed measurements of 73 horses and comparing their findings with the horses' official handicap ratings. Dr John Manning of the University's Department of Evolutionary Biology selected the horses from the Epsom area and checked the measurements of their knees, teeth, cheekbones, ears and other points, and concluded that the final results were so accurate that the chances of them being coincidental were one in ten thousand. The biologists believe that 'fluctuating asymmetry' could provide the

---

Steve Donoghue won his sixth Derby in the **one hundred and forty-sixth** running of the race as Manna became the 1925 winner.

key to picking out potentially top class performers at yearling sales by checking the extent to which their right sides match with the left.

It was literally a case of 20/1 'bar' when one of the oddest racing tales of recent years unfolded in the American north-west in August 1994.

A stranger, claiming to be jockey Sam Shirley, visited or telephoned the majority of the bars in Spokane, whose local track is Playfair. He told bar owners and drinkers the same story. His wife had been in the bar a few days previously with friends who were going to give her a lift home. She had decided to leave early and asked the barman to call her a cab, which he had done. When the other couple left later they were involved in a car crash and killed. The barman had therefore saved his wife's life and he wanted everyone to know how grateful he was by telling them that the horse he was to ride in a five furlong sprint, Why Dilly Dally, would win. The horse had little form and opened up at 20/1, only to plunge in the betting down to 9/5 favourite as everyone who had been tipped the 'good thing' rushed to get on. The horse finished stone last.

Acquainted with the story, Sam Shirley denied all knowledge of it. Was it a cunning plan to lengthen the odds of another horse or horses in the race? No evidence was forthcoming. Spooky!

SLINGING LE SLANG EN FRANÇAIS

British racing slang has been given wide currency. But what about a guide for those intrepid Brit racegoers (les rosbifs) who venture across the water, courtesy of Le Chunnel to see, for example, L'Arc de Triomphe?

What strange words and phrases can they expect to hear as their cheval (horse) passes le disque (winning post)?

Well, on arrival at l'hippodrome (racecourse), you may be given a number of conseils (tips) and want to check les cotes (odds) before deciding which of them to parier (bet) on at le guichet (betting window). Le favori (favourite) could be at tout seul (evens) or perhaps toi et moi (2/1), avec l'aimant 3/1), possibly poing (5/1) or even à-la-coq (9/1). Maybe you fancy an outsider at les deux bossus (33/1).

The racing will be on le plat (flat) or la course de haies (hurdles) or le steeple-chase (guess!).

La poisse (bad luck) is universal for punters (joueurs), so listen out for news that your horse is tocard (useless, a dead loss), the victim of a réclamation (objection) or enquête (stewards' enquiry) – or may even have been rétrogradé (disqualified).

If you do manage to back un lauréat (winner) then

Pat Eddery won his first jockey title in 1974 with
one hundred and forty-eight winners.

enjoy your bonne chance (good luck) and head for le bar, where you may be able to afford to boire (drink) some excellent champagne.

WADDA MISTAKEA TO MAKEA

American jockey Kent Desmormeaux made probably the most expensive mistake ever recorded by a jockey when 176,619 racegoers saw him drop his hands on the favourite for the world's richest race, the 1993 Japan Cup. Run at Fuchu, Tokyo, Desmormeaux had mistaken the winning post during a race the day before and, incredibly, did it again when his mount Kotashaan was challenging the leader, Legacy World. He stood up in the saddle, briefly, slowing his horse's momentum and finished up second. 'I feel very ashamed. I made a big mistake,' he told reporters – before being fined just £300, having cost connections of the Dick Mandella trained runner somewhat more to say nothing of the percentage of the £215 million wagered on the race, which had been staked on Kotashaan.

Mistakes of another kind produced mega winnings for two punters in November 1995. One anonymous jackpot winner at the Breeders Cup was over 9 million pounds better off after wrongly backing number 11 instead of number 1 in the last race, while Hong Kong gambler Larry Yung apparently backed 100/1 outsider Best Of Luck by mistake, and promptly gave away his

---

Robert Massey rode his first winner, Stylus, at Leicester in February 1993 – at **one hundred and fifty** to one.

£3.3million accumulative winnings to fund the education of students from the Chinese mainland.

Nottingham punter Philip Tilson's Tricast (first three in order) bet on the 1993 Derby with Ladbrokes was a catalogue of mistakes. Firstly, they weren't actually offering the bet, which would have paid out £116,000 with the bookies who were. Then Tilson refused to accept an offer of £33,870 as advised by the *Sporting Life*. Instead he went to arbitration where he was ruled to be entitled to just £728 – and it then transpired that as he was only 17 at the time the bet was placed he was entitled to nothing other than the refund of his £4 stake money!

CLASSIFIED INFORMATION

In November 1994 a lonely jump jockey took out an advert in the personal columns of *The Times*, declaring: 'National Hunt Jockey, mid 30s, blue eyes, curly hair, seeks attractive 18-21 year old. I shall be at Newbury racecourse for The Hennessy Gold Cup on Nov 26. Wear a red carnation and meet me outside the weighing room at 12.30.' Once the story got out, more media turned up at the appointed hour than would-be jockey companions.

Lambourn trainer John Hills had more success in December 1995 when he advertised in the *Sporting Life* for a 'charming young lady for dinner date tonight with a leading young Lambourn NH trainer.' In fact, the ad was designed to produce a dining companion for Hills' pal, trainer Charlie Egerton, and it worked as Grantham trainer Jane Bower responded and later reported: 'Mr Egerton wasn't rude, just danced and played the guitar with a stick of celery in his mouth.'

In the States, readers of the daily *Racing Form* were stunned to see an April 1995 ad, reading: 'Affluent race fan with finish line box at Santa Anita, Hollywood and Del Mar Turf Club, seeks slim, fit, sophisticated female, 25-35 (no kids) to share fun times and more.'

Fred Darling trained and Freddie Fox rode Cameronian who, in 1931, won Epsom Derby number **one hundred and fifty-two** at odds of 7/2.

WAGER BELIEVE IT!?

'I picked up a paper, looked at a race and the only jockey I had heard of was Willie Carson. So I asked my mate to put £200 on it for me. It won at 7/1, but my mate only put on £100, thinking he'd save me £100 as he thought it couldn't win.' Former Liverpool star turned Swansea manager, Jan Molby on his first ever bet, struck in 1988.

'The way the betting's going we're going to have no winner at all – no horse will be first past the post.' Typically over the top comment from an excited John McCririck, bemoaning the lack of activity in the betting ring prior to the off of the 3.05 at Sandown on 2 April 1996 which, strange to relate, did produce a winner!

'I remember betting my mother I could eat an omelette with 12 eggs in it – I was very sick.' Charlie Brooks who, it must be said, has never struck me as being an egg-head, recalling his first (presumably, losing) wager.

April the Fifth was the 1932 winner of Epsom Derby number **one hundred and fifty-three** at 100/6, owned by actor Tom Walls.

'Don't mistake an ante-post bet for sheer greed. It is simply a way of prolonging life, and I have always believed in that corny old superstition that a man holding an ante-post voucher never dies before the race itself is run.' Jeffrey Bernard. In which case I think I'll take out a bet now on the result of the Derby in the year 2099!

'He won on Rocktor at Towcester. I thought he would. Rocktor's form figures were PP-PPP. Classic Bank Holiday Monday form.' The *Sporting Life*'s phlegmatic David Ashforth with a perceptive observation about an Easter 1996 winner.

'I don't follow particular horses – although horses I back seem to.' Rueful former soccer supremo Tommy 'more clubs than Nick Faldo' Docherty who went on to tell the *Sporting Life* Weekender in April 1996: 'I prefer to bet with bookmakers and go straight in for the kill, so win bets are my favourites. Unfortunately, I'm usually the one who gets killed.'

Otto Madden scored the second of his three jockey titles in 1903 with **one hundred and fifty-four** winners.

'If I were a serious punter I would go racing wearing a Walkman, pick out and back the horses I fancied and in no circumstances whatsoever talk to a trainer.' Red-shirted trainer Jack Berry on the dangers of paying too much heed to the opinions of his ilk.

'The horse doesn't know he's the outsider, and I'm not going to tell him.' But someone less tactful than trainer Clive Brittain did get to 100/1 shot Needle Gun before the start of the 1996 Dubai World Cup to whisper in his ear that he was unlikely to take a hand in the finish – he was 7th out of 11.

'I haven't had a bet on a horse in all the 35 years I've been in racing.' Trainer Terry Casey who must have wished he'd broken that habit, after his Rough Quest won the 1996 Grand National.

'I don't involve myself in betting, I think it's for nutters.' Frank Bruno, who apparently sees no element of nuttiness involved in twice entering a boxing ring in order to have his head hammered by Mike Tyson.

Doug Smith's **one hundred and fifty-five** 1956 winners
were enough to give him his third jockey title.

'Go down to the paddock and back anything that appeals to you, anything that gives you a wink – unless it is Jamie Osborne, in which case it means that he can see all the way down your cleavage.' Winner-finding advice from former jump jockey and former husband of Jenny, Richard Pitman, to female novice punters at the 1996 Cheltenham Festival.

'If anybody had told me in 1971 that in 1996 the industry would still bet 8/13, 10/11 or 15/8, I wouldn't have believed them.' Well, retiring Chairman of the Betting Offices Licensees' Association, Don Bruce, you can have 20/21 with me that these archaic odds are still around in a hundred years' time.

'I'm burying my husband this afternoon, but I just had to have a little bet before the funeral.' Answer from lady in a betting-shop to a London cabbie who enquired why she was clad all in black. Presumably she'd found a dead cert.

'Anyone who bets before the day,when the draw and its effects are known, has to be a five-iron short of a full set.' Golf-loving *Sporting Life* writer Jeremy Chapman on the difficulties of unravelling the Lincoln Handicap.

1935 saw hot favourite, Bahram, at 5/4 win the
one hundred and fifty-sixth Derby for trainer Frank Butters.

Leicester staged a card which attracted **one hundred and fifty seven** runners during 1949, a record which stood for six years.

'My Dad always used to tell me that betting is a mug's game. But I won't ever give it up completely. It would be like being on a diet, which meant you could never have another glass of Guinness. I would probably strangle myself first.' Former Monkee and now winning amateur jockey, Davy Jones.

'There is an immutable rule in betting that if you beat the odds by more than half, the beast in question either falls over, contracts Green Monkey Disease, or is assassinated by some raving loon.' Alastair Down, who often beats the odds, but seldom backs a winner, looking for sympathy from readers of the *Sporting Life* Weekender.

'Association football and racing, they are the great interests for the average man. The first because he likes it, and the second because he can bet on it, too.' MP turned political commentator on the box and would be BHB member, Brian Walden, apparently oblivious to the fact that up to £5 million is gambled on the FA Cup Final and that the 1994 World Cup produced a UK betting turnover in the region of £75 million.

Mid-Day Sun, ridden by M Beary, won the
one hundred and fifty-eightth Derby at 100/7 in 1937.

'Now is the time to bet like men.' Inspired advice from the late racing writer Richard Baerlein who, well before the actual race, was imploring readers to take advantage of the double-figure odds then available on Shergar winning the 1981 Derby – which he duly did at the prohibitive price of 10/11.

'It was fantastic, we've blown £10,000 and when it's someone like Channel 4's money it's a very, very good feeling. Spiritually I think we've won.' Bookies are always happy with punters who are happy to accept spiritual winnings – comedian Mark Thomas, though, gambled the whole budget for the final episode of his Channel 4 series of spring 1996, on an unplaced nag at Doncaster races. It was all filmed for the show and, to make up the deficit, the final programme was recorded in Thomas's front room.

'At Beijing (racecourse) there is a Tote board with notices on either side reminding you that betting is a crime.' With double standards like that the Chinese should have no problem in continuing to enjoy the benefits of capitalist Hong Kong whilst officially deploring them. Guy Watkins, the Chief Executive of the Hong Kong Jockey Club, spilled the beans on the Chinese hypocrisy in October 1995.

Scot Willie Carson rode **one hundred and fifty-nine** winners *en route* to his title triumph of 1983, his last of five.

'Every Lottery ticket is at least a trier. The same cannot be said of every horse and greyhound.' True enough, but equally it cannot be denied that every Lottery ticket is returned at odds so much below its true value that even the biggest winners are being ripped off. Paul Dwyer made his point in a letter to the *Sporting Life* in September 1995.

'I thought I was a goner but the thought of all those punters anxious to give me their money kept me going.' Bookmaker David Pipe, father of champion jump jockey Martin, after he recovered, having stopped breathing during an operation which, presumably, was not carried out by a punter.

'Dear Bastard. You could not tip more rubbish if London Weekend bought you a forklift truck.' Fan letter sent by *Daily Telegraph* reader to Lord Oaksey.

'No organ in the world works better than a successful bookie's nose. Fill him with malt whisky and douse him in a vat of garlic and he can still smell a rat four streets away, side-stepping a diesel-fuelled bus.' A rather conservative estimate of a turf accountant's capacity to spot a dodgy 'un from writer John Thicknesse of the *Evening Standard*.

Jockey, Aiden Wall, reportedly weighed **one hundred and sixty** pounds when partnering Release the Beast to win at Roscommon in September 1991. Nine days later when they won at Dundalk, he was down to 144lbs.

'The majority of accidents are from the public falling when rushing to the bookies to get their money.' St John ambulance man Glynn Reeve who was based at Salisbury racecourse in May 1995, and who added: 'Coronaries are common from cheering home a winner.'

'A man's gotta make at least one bet every day, else he would be walking around lucky and never know it.' US trainer Jimmy Jones.

'If I knew what horse would win, I wouldn't be riding, I'd be betting.' US jockey Don Brumfield.

'No horse can go as fast as the money you put on it.' Cautionary warning from US writer Earl Wilson.

'I gamble on the punter rather than the horse. I don't care about the horse's reputation, if I think the backer is a born loser I will stand his bet for a fortune.' Aussie bookie Bill Waterhouse.

Otto Madden scored **one hundred and sixty-one** victories to claim the first of four jockey championships in 1898.

'When it comes to protecting punters' interests the biggest non-trier seems to be the Jockey Club.' Nick Mordin.

'Win or lose, it is always a terrible day for the racecourse bookie . . . things aren't what they used to be, he can tell you . . . The bookie, like the British farmer, is a fund of pessimism.' Victoria Mather spotting the betting man's essential lack of optimism.

'There is no doubt that, during the last couple of years, the winning margins in some races have been longer or shorter than they would have been if spread betting had not been invented.' What *could* David Ashforth be insinuating?

'I have occasionally used my crystal ball to "see" results of races. Or asked the runes to spell out a winning name. But I don't think this is very sporting. So I only do it when I truly need to win.' Mystic Meg.

Lester Piggott's **one hundred and sixty-two** total was sufficient to win him the jockey championship in both 1970 and 71.

'My mode of transport is a bike – and I even got mugged on that recently, so I believe I put the "you've never seen a poor bookmaker" myth into a much clearer perspective.' Village bookie Tony Ambrose.

'The message for everyone involved with the sport is simple. If you care about racing boycott the Lottery.' Greg Wood.

'When people go racing and don't bet it is only a matter of time before the novelty wears off and they don't go racing.' Yes, yes, I *know* that Tom Kelly of the Betting Office Licensees' Association would say that – but, think about it, he's right.

'The National Lottery is trash, a sleazy low life Treasury rip-off, a scummy exercise in triple taxation that demeans and infantilizes everything it touches.' Now, do you imagine the *Independent*'s Brian Appleyard is pro or anti the Lottery?

Lester Piggott won **one hundred and sixty-three** times on the way to his seventh jockey title in 1969.

Joe Mercer's only jockey title came in 1979 when he rode
one hundred and sixty-four winners.

'I needed something to get up for in the mornings.' £1.9m Lottery winner Alan Baker, former betting shop manager, who became a bookie at Ramsgate dogs after his big win – and lost £3,000 on his first night.

'Even when you know, you never know.' Cautionary betting advice to punters from *Sporting Life Weekender* pundit Bob Toseland.

'I think racecourse bookies are wonderful. Perhaps we should have a flag day for them?' Actor Melvyn *It Ain't Half Hot, Mum* Hayes. And he was speaking before the Dettori seven went in.

'New Zealanders will bet on anything that moves. And, if it doesn't move, they'll kick it and bet on when it will move.' BBC Political Editor and racing enthusiast, Robin Oakley.

'If you can sell a horse at 6/4, you're a fool to lay 13/8.' The greatest bookmaker of all, William Hill, recalled by Peter O'Sullevan; making a comment which is fundamental to the understanding of a bookie's philosophy but which is grasped by few punters.

Pat Eddery chalked up his ninth flat jockey title with **one hundred and sixty-five** winners in 1991.

'Betting is an emotional as well as a cerebral activity, in which a punter's pride operates to the bookmaker's advantage.' Peter O'Sullevan.

'Time is time and form is form, but I am convinced that there is some mysterious alliance between them that is still undiscovered.' Founder of punters' aid, Timeform, Phil Bull, in a 1943 letter to form expert Dick Whitford with whom he would eventually team up to create the 'Black Book' organization.

'Imagine . . . strike the bet on Friday, watch the horse lose on Saturday, and cancel the wager any time before the following Thursday.' Tom Kelly of the Betting Office Licencees' Association, who spotted and quashed an EU draft directive on distance selling which 'Had it been implemented it would have given credit punters seven days to reconsider after placing a bet.'

'I first became interested in racing at school. A boy was severely punished for running a book and it seemed to me that anything the authorities were so much against – drinking and sex were the other things that made them angry – must be worth pursuing.'

A record **one hundred and sixty-six** runners competed on a six race card at Windsor in November 1955.

Writer Jeffrey Bernard explaining how he began betting at the age of 15 in 1947.

'We found women tended to out-perform men and the figures were statistically significant. I should think most men in betting shops would say this is ridiculous, but we have no axe to grind. It rather surprised us as well.' Dr Alistair Bruce of Nottingham University's school of management and finance, who in March 1996 announced the findings of their joint survey of 1,200 men and women's high street betting shop gambling habits, concluding a little confusingly, 'Men and women appear to perceive risk differently. Men took the riskier bet, women the insurance (each-way) option. Men go for riskier bet types, but on safer horses.'

You can't bet in China – but you can 'guess' the winners of horse races. When racing resumed there after a forty-year gap in 1992 the authorities got round the ideological problem of gambling being prohibited by introducing to the track 'Horse Racing Intelligence contests' with punters who successfully 'guessed' winners collecting their winnings from Prize

Tom Loates took his first flat jockey title in 1889, riding **one hundred and sixty-seven** winners.

Redemption Counters. How will fanatical Hong Kong gamblers react to that when the Chinese take over? We can only guess!

MY FAVOURITE RACEHORSES . . . .

1 **Sea Pigeon** . . . Talented, versatile, game, charismatic
2 **Baulking Green** . . . Prolific hunter chaser
3 **Sharpo** . . . Top sprinter who won on the day my first son was born
4 **Red Rum** . . . No explanation necessary
5 **Bird's Nest** . . . Lovable rogue
6 **Morley Street** . . . Tough as teak
7 **Moor Lane** . . . Lightning fast but barely stayed 5 furlongs
8 **Night Nurse** . . . See Sea Pigeon comments
9 **Lammtarra** . . . Just how good was he?
10 **Desert Orchid** . . . For the buzz his very appearance created

MY FAVOURITE JOCKEYS

1 **John Francome**
2 **Steve Cauthen**
3 **Frankie Dettori**
4 **Lester Piggott**
5 **Jamie Osborne**

MY FAVOURITE TRAINERS

1 **Peter Easterby**
2 **Jack Berry**
3 **Jenny Pitman**
4 **Gay Kelleway**
5 **Martin Pipe**

French-trained My Love was the 1948 winner of Epsom Derby number **one hundred and sixty-nine** for the Aga Khan at 100/9.

Lester Piggott won the jockey championship for the first time in 1960
with **one hundred and seventy** winners.

MY FAVOURITE RACECOURSES

1 **Les Landes, Jersey**
2 **Ascot**
3 **Sandown**
4 **Musselburgh**
5 **Goodwood**

THINGS YOU DIDN'T KNOW ABOUT RACEHORSES

- In a race a horse can breathe up to 150 times a minute.

- Thoroughbreds can travel at 37-38mph.

- Horse's strides measure from 5.5-7.3m.

- The average racehorse has a body mass of 446 kg, of which 42.9 per cent is muscle, 9.7 per cent blood.

- At rest a racehorse's heart beats 36-42 times per minute; flat out, from 210-240.

- A racehorse can go from 0-42mph in 2.5secs and six strides – a powerful car will accelerate from 0-60 in 3.7s.

- A mare's gestation period is eleven months.

- A virile stallion can become a sire between 60-70 times in a year, perhaps 600 in a lifetime.

Doping accusations following Hill House's 1967 Schweppes Gold Trophy victory were dropped after a **one hundred and seventy-one** day enquiry.

AUSSIE SLANG

BIRD . . . Certainty
BOAT RACE . . . Crooked race
BRICK . . . $20
DESPERATE . . . A punter
GORILLA . . . $1,000
MONTY . . . Certainty
OUT THE GATE . . . Market Drifter
PERSUADER . . . Whip
COP A PRAT . . . To suffer interference in running
ROUGHIE . . . Outsider
RUN DEAD . . . Non-trier
WHIPPING THEM IN . . . Finishing last

OF COURSE

The appropriately named Finger Lakes racecourse in the States was the first track given permission to open a massage salon in its members' enclosure in 1994.

Rio de Janeiro's racecourse launched a new state-of-the-art beer dispenser in its El Turf bar in 1995. Four miles of tubing and a computerized billing system were the highlights of the equipment, made in New Zealand. But when customs officials heard about this they could find no record of import duty – so they confiscated it.

It's not official – but I think the world's longest racetrack name must belong to Madagascar's 'Hippodrome Fandrosoana D'Ambohimandroso' – unless you know better. Shortest? Now defunct Wye would be hard to beat.

Racing at Dusseldorf was abandoned in May 1996 for one of the most bizarre reasons ever recorded – the death of a high-wire motor cyclist's female assistant. She was performing at one of the sideshows put on to entertain racegoers.

Australian track Ballarat, near Melbourne, witnessed a unique event in November 1994 when five members of the same family – all licensed jockeys – raced against each other in a race. Patrick, 19, came out on top, riding the winner, leaving Therese, 24, Maree, 22, Bernadette, 21 and Andrew 15 trailing behind.

TEN FEMALE FIRSTS

1691 . . . *The Chester Recorder* noted that a 'Mrs Morte was the winning rider in a local horse race.'

1904 . . . Elwood was the first Kentucky Derby runner and winner – owned by a woman, Mrs Charles Durnell.

1915 . . . Lady Nelson became the first female owner of a Grand National winner with her Ally Sloper.

1918 . . . Lady James Douglas was the first female owner of a Derby winner when Gainsborough won – the horse, by the way, was named after a railway station, not the painter! Her Ladyship was described as 'a short, erect, stoutly-built lady attired in spats, a severely cut coat and skirt, a masculine bow tie and a hat totally devoid, perhaps intentionally so, of feminine allurement.'

1982 . . . The Princess Royal became the first lady royal to ride a winner when Gulfland scored at Redcar.

1986 . . . Caroline Beasley was the first female winner over the Aintree fences, riding Eliogarty to victory in the Foxhunters' Chase.

1987 . . . Gee Armytage rode the appropriately named Gee–A (no relation) becoming the first woman to ride a Cheltenham Festival winner.

Doug Smith, who retired in 1967 with 3111 winners to his credit, rode **one hundred and seventy-three** of them in his best year, 1947.

1988 . . . Morag Chalmers became, at Hamilton Park, the first female Clerk of the Course anywhere.

1988 . . . Caroline Lee became the first woman to ride in the French Derby, finishing tenth on Face Nord.

1989 . . . Pamela Rouse, daughter of jockey Brian, became the first Page Three girl jockey, appearing more out of than in a set of jockey silks in the *People* newspaper.

UPPER CLASS DOWNERS

King James I paid the royal sum of £154 in 1605 for a new horse expected to prove a champion. However, the Duke of Newcastle later reported: 'When he came to run, every horse beat him.'

King George IV was assaulted at Ascot racecourse in the late 18th century by a one-legged sailor who lobbed a stone at the monarch, damaging his hat.

The Duke of Richmond's Dandizette clearly won the 1824 Goodwood Stakes, only for judge Charles Greville to completely overlook the far-side runner in favour of two near-side contestants, who were placed first and second.

Queen Mother's Devon Loch collapsed inexplicably on the run in when clear in the 1956 Grand National.

Lord Oaksey (then plain old John Lawrence) was fined £25 after jumping the second last clear at Cheltenham in amateurs' race, only to turn around fearing he'd taken the wrong course – he hadn't.

Prince Charles lost his first winner as an owner-breeder when Devil's Elbow, successful in a Worcester hurdles race in 1988, was disqualified after a test revealed prohibited substances.

Princess Royal fell at the first on Cannon Class in a November 1988 Windsor Chase.

Aga Khan's Aliysa was disqualified as the winner of the 1989 Oaks, leading to his boycott of the British turf.

William Hastings-Bass, Royal trainer, was fined for failing to allow The Queen's Christmas Tree to run on its merits at Newmarket in November 1990.

Elizabeth Major, daughter of PM John, made her racing debut at Huntingdon, only to fall off as she passed the post.

HORSE LAUGHS ? THE CORNIER THE BETTER . . .

If gambling is so great, how come you never see horses betting on people?

Two jockeys were riding at Southwell. One asked the other: 'Do you prefer grass or fibresand?' 'I don't know,' replied the other. 'I've never smoked fibresand.'

'He's done everything we've asked of him at home,' the trainer told the owner. 'Excellent,' replied the owner, 'and have you asked him to win this afternoon?'

The racehorse walked up to the bookie and asked for a tenner on himself. The bookie just stared. 'What's up – never heard of a talking horse?' 'Certainly. I just can't believe you think you'll win.'

What's the definition of a pessimist? An optimist on the way home from the races.

'I came by the racetrack today, but it was closed,' said comedian W C Fields, 'so I just shoved all my money through the gate.'

In horse racing there's nothing so uncertain as a certainty.

Tony McCoy landed his first jump jockey title for season 1995-96, with **one hundred and seventy-five** winners to his credit.

Then there was the gambling-mad vet who crossed a racehorse with a giraffe to get a runner which would never be beaten in a photo-finish.

The beautiful girl asked the librarian, 'Can you recommend something I'll enjoy?' 'Do you like Dick Francis?' asked the librarian. 'Of course I do,' she said. 'But my name isn't Frances.'

There are many who consider that the form book should be written in braille – for the benefit of the stewards.

Then there was the poorly jockey – he was in a stable condition.

New book – *The Unluckiest Punter* by Mr Winner.

Jockey Gordon Richards on becoming a Sir: 'I'm the shortest knight of the year.'

A racehorse – the only creature capable of taking thousands for a ride at the same time.

How to make a small fortune by backing horses – start with a large one.

A bookie's favourite time of day? Twenty-five to one.

'I hope I break even today,' said the punter. 'I need the money.'

Then there was the world's worst burglar, who broke into the bookies – and lost £500.

My bookie and I are like Siamese twins – we're joined at the wallet.

A WEATHER EYE ON RACING

The Drought of summer 1989 saw Uttoxeter call in a Red Indian rain-man to encourage a downpour.

A Blizzard poured down as the 1901 Grand National was won by Grudon, whose shrewd trainer had rubbed butter into the horse's

The most prolific winning horse to race in Britain was Catherina who, from 1833-41, won 79 of **one hundred and seventy-six** races.

hooves to prevent snow from balling there.

Thick mist allowed jockey Sylvester Carmouche to miss out a circuit of a race at Louisiana in 1990 before joining in and winning easily. He was jailed for thirty days.

Thunderstorms were to blame for one fatality at Royal Ascot in 1930 and two more in 1955 – all were struck by lightning.

Sunstroke kept Gordon Richards out of the saddle from 9-25 July, 1949 – he contracted it at, of all places, Ascot.

Violent wind and a sudden darkness caused such havoc at a meeting at Crosby Marsh near Liverpool in 1733 that racegoers were still unaccounted for next day.

Sun in his horse's eyes was jockey Tim Reed's excuse to sceptical Sedgefield racegoers in December 1993 when his mount Celtic Song turned in a disappointing display.

Fog was to blame for the first abandonment of all-weather racing because of weather conditions, which happened at Southwell in November 1989.

Bad weather over Christmas 1985 meant that Catterick re-staged its festive-themed meeting, complete with race titles, including the Stuffed Turkey Handicap, in August 1986.

An earthquake caused scaffolding at Santa Anita, US, to fall from the grandstand, killing a 35-year-old woman in June 1991.

NATIONAL FIRSTS

First horse to die in the National – Dictator. Fell at first, 1839.

First winning jockey to end up in debtors' prison – 1842's Gay Lad rider, Tom Olliver.

French-trained Lavandin was the winner of 1956's
one hundred and seventy-seventh Derby
for trainer Alec Head at 7/1.

First winner to walk to Aintree from Grimsby – and back again afterwards, Cure All in 1845.

First horse to fall into the Mersey whilst being unloaded from a steamer prior to the race – Sir Arthur, unplaced, in 1848.

First losing jockey to offer winner a bribe on the run-in: Capt D'Arcy who promised £4,000 to T Cunningham in 1849 if he'd 'take a pull' on Peter Simple.

First National favourite to be 'got at' – Miss Mowbray, unable to run in 1854 after her leg was attacked.

First jockey fatality – James Wynn on O'Connell in 1862, only hours after hearing of his sister's death.

First favourite killed before even jumping a fence – Chimney Sweep who, in 1868, ran into a boulder.

First dream winner – The Lamb, in 1871, whose owner Lord Poulet 'saw' Tommy Pickernell ride the horse to victory in his sleep and then went out and booked him for the ride.

First Punch and Judy man to own a winner – E Brayley in 1872, whose Casse Tete showed 'the way to do it'.

First winning jockey to retire after the owner accused him of telling all his friends to 'get on' thus destroying the odds – John Richardson, who won on 5/1 favourite Reugny in 1874.

First stone-drunk winning jockey – Tommy Pickernell on Pathfinder who, in 1875, before the off had to ask which way he should be facing.

First winner to end up on the West End stage – Voluptuary, who starred in The Prodigal Daughter after winning in 1884.

First winning jockey to have a Kenyan waterfall named after him – Capt. Roddy Owen, army officer who died in Africa but is remembered by the Owen Falls. Won on Father O'Flynn in 1892.

Paul Fredericks, 19, rode his first winner on his third ride in June 1996 when 33/1 shot, Percy Parrot, scored at Pontefract, paying **one hundred and seventy-eight** to one on the Tote.

Scobie Breasley booted home **one hundred and seventy-nine** winners in 1962 – the highest of his four title winning totals.

First winner to be shipwrecked en route to the race – New Zealand-bred 1904 winner Moifaa.

First winning jockey paid £300 NOT to ride for a fortnight before the 1905 race to avoid injury – Frank Mason on Kirkland.

First winner to have regularly pulled a hotel bus to and from Towcester Station – Rubio, 1908, also first US–bred winner.

First official complaint from RSPCA about cruelty of race came in 1922.

First jockey to ride two runners in race – Bill O'Neill in 1924 fell from Libretto, mounted Conjuror II, caught Libretto, remounted him – and fell again.

First 70,000/1 winner – Emilio Scala in 1931 who won £354,544 for 50p Irish Hospitals Sweepstake ticket on 100/1 winner Grakle.

First time race won by two Furlongs – 1935 when Frank Furlong, jockey, and Noel Furlong, owner-trainer, were connections of Reynoldstown.

First England soccer skipper to own runner – Emlyn Hughes' 1979 faller, Wayward Scott.

First owner to will winner to jockey – veteran Jim Noel's 1987 Maori Venture to Steve Knight.

AND THE LAST THINGS YOU EVER WANTED TO KNOW:

Last moustachioed jockey to win National – Mr Campbell on The Soarer in 1896.

Last professional boxer to ride in race – Johnny Broome, knocked out when Eagle fell in 1848.

Great champion jockey, Fred Archer, born in 1857, had **one hundred and eighty** mounts as a fifteen-year-old, winning on 27 of them.

Last grey to win, Nicolaus Silver in 1961.

Last French-trained winner, Cortolvin in 1867.

Last to train first and second, Fred Withington in 1908.

Last 100/1 winner, Foinavon in 1967.

Last 13-year-old winner, Sgt Murphy in 1923.

Last 5-year-old winner, Lutteur, 1909.

Last to win at sixth attempt – Frigate, 1889.

Last one-eyed winner – Glenside, 1911.

Last 48-year-old winning jockey, Dick Saunders on Grittar in 1982.

Last 17-year-old winning jockey, Bruce Hobbs on Battleship in 1938.

ELEVEN CELEBRITIES WHO ENJOYED MIXED FORTUNES IN RACING:

Freddie Starr bought his Grand National winner Miinnehoma at auction – bidding by sticking his tongue out.

Percy Sugden of Coronation Street or – to be accurate, actor Bill Waddington – owned a racehorse named, excruciatingly, Lucy Lastic.

Sir Gary Sobers, the West Indian cricket ace, backed 10/1, 20/1 and 4/1 winners in one day in August 1968 then, by way of a celebration, went out to bat against Glamorgan – and thumped a record six sixes in one over.

David Coleman emphatically did not balls up a question of sport when, in the BBC Grand National Sweepstake in 1967, he drew shock 100/1 winner Foinavon.

Graham Greene, the fabled author, went to the races at Brighton

Lester Piggott and Noel Murless teamed up to win Derby running number **one hundred and eighty-one** as 7/1 shot, St Paddy, won the 1960 race.

whilst researching his early novel, *Brighton Rock* – only to fail to back the 10/1 winner of that name whilst there.

Paul Daniels entered his own horse That's Magic, in the race he sponsored at Redcar – it did him 'not a lot' of good, though, by finishing fifteenth of eighteen.

Bing Crosby was part-owner of 1965 Derby runner-up Meadow Court which went on to win the Irish Derby whereupon, as the horse returned to the winners' enclosure, Bing regaled the crowd with an impromptu rendition of 'When Irish Eyes are Smiling'.

Paul McCartney bought his father a horse called Drake's Drum – and led it into the winners' enclosure at Aintree in 1966.

Sting was persuaded by a gang of Irish builders at his home to buy a horse – called Sweetcal, it won for him at 33/1.

George Formby must have had more than a little ukulele in his hand whilst working as an apprentice jockey in 1915.

SECONDS OUT, ELEVEN RACING PUNCH-UPS

Round One . . . Zapp! . . . In 1986 US super-jock, Julie Krone, walloped Miguel Rujano with a right hook after he had lashed her across the face with his whip during a race at Monmouth.

Round Two . . . Pow! . . . The Krone-Rujano feud flared up again when the pair met at a swimming pool – and Krone smashed Rujano over the head with a chair.

Round Three . . . Bam! . . . Jenny Pitman and jockey Jamie Osborne indulged in a catch-weight bout in 1990, during which the former won a points verdict with a single blow to the head.

Round Four . . . Crash! . . . Jamie Osborne was in the firing line again as he lost a tooth when he and Billy Morris disagreed during a Newbury weighing room conversation in February 1992.

Willie Carson won his third jockey championship with
one hundred and eighty-two winners in 1978.

Pat Eddery's 1988 score of **one hundred and eighty-three**
winners gave him his sixth jockey title.

Round Five . . . Biff! . . . After a hard-fought race at Suffolk Downs, US, in June 1993, Dodie Duys, 33, and Carl Gambardella, 53, came to blows. They were separated, only for Gambardella to sneak into the ladies' shower room and attack Duys. Both were suspended for 15 days but, at least, it must have been a clean fight.

Round Six . . . Bash! . . . Accused of a lack of patriotism for training horses for French owners in the late 1870s at his Newmarket stables at a time when the two nations were not on the best of terms, Triple Crown winning trainer Thomas Jennings came to blows with his accuser and fellow trainer Mat Dawson.

Round Seven . . . Bop! . . . Steward Scott Whitman was left with a bleeding nose after stepping between brawling jockeys Gary Skinner and Steven Maskiell in 1989, at Hobart, Australia.

Round Eight . . . Thwack! . . . Objecting to the excessive whipping which he had inflicted on her fourth-placed Turkey Buzzard in the 1921 Grand National, owner Mrs M Hollins hammered jockey Captain Geoffrey Bennet around the paddock – beating him with her brolly.

Round Nine . . . Thump! . . . Deliberate jostling during a race between Sam Chifney senior (1753-1807) and Dick Goodisson (1750-1817) escalated into a punch-up. They were separated and agreed to fight it out for real in a proper boxing ring for a 25 guinea stake. Goodisson won the bout.

Round Ten . . . Blam! . . . Racegoers, jockeys and officials at Garfield Park, Chicago, raced for cover as the course was raided by armed police in 1892 as part of a feud between rival tracks. Garfield's owner James M Browne killed two cops before he himself was shot. Garfield Park, you'll not be surprised to learn, was closed down for good.

Round Eleven . . . Bosh! . . . 29-year-old Kieran Fallon dragged fellow rider Stuart Webster from his mount as the pair finished a race at Beverley in September 1994. The pair later emerged from the weighing room with facial wounds.

Weighing out at an incredible **one hundred and eighty-four** pounds, Mr Theo West of Louth, finished third on Cornafulla at Market Rasen in October 1934.

WHIP IT OUT . . . WHIP CONTROVERSIES ARE NOTHING NEW

1607 . . . 'In your right hande you must have a long rodde finely ash-growne, so that the small ende thereof bee hardly so great as a round packe-thread, inasmuch that when you move or shake it, the noyse thereof may be lowde and sharpe.' Gervase Markham on the whip in *English Horseman*.

1738 . . . A donkey race run at Newcastle included the condition that all runners were to be ridden by chimney sweeps who should use their brushes as whips.

18th century . . . Jamie Duff of Edinburgh spotted a gap in the rules when he entered a race at Leigh which he contested carrying a whip – but without the assistance of a horse. He finished tailed off 'a poor last'.

1915 . . . Jumps rider Martin Gubb, discovering that organizers of a Worcestershire point-to-point had banned whips and spurs, inserted tin tacks into his riding boots instead.

1935 . . . Jockey J Hickey won a race on Speed On at Folkestone carrying, instead of a whip, a rattle. Their use was later banned.

1955 . . . Aussie jockey Bill Attrill was banned for ten years after being discovered using a battery-powered whip in Adelaide.

1964 . . . Terry Biddlecombe, riding The Pouncer at Stratford, dropped his whip. After unsuccessfully offering a tenner for a replacement he leaned across and snatched one, proceeding to ride his mount to victory.

1979 . . . Battling for second place at Deauville against Alain Lequeux, Lester Piggott, who had dropped his whip earlier in the race, leant across and grabbed the Frenchman's, going on to finish second only to be demoted and suspended for twenty days.

1983 . . . Aussie racing writer Jeremy J Matters wrote: 'The battery whip is used by jamming the handle of the whip into the horse's

---

Derby number **one hundred and eighty-five** was run in 1964 and 15/8 chance, Santa Claus, trained in Ireland by J Rogers, came out on top.

neck. The battery in the handle is activated when the metal tip at the end is depressed.'

1984 . . . New Zealand jockey David Walsh won on Colman – carrying TWO whips – the practice was immediately banned by local stewards.

1996 . . . The first three jockeys home in the 2,000 Guineas were all suspended for excessive use of the whip.

DEAD-HEATS . . .

New equipment could make dead-heats a thing of the past. Here are some from the past:

1797 . . . The first ever Quadruple Dead Heat as Honest Harry, Miss Decoy, Beningborough and Petoria flashed past the post together at Bogside on 7 June.

1828 . . . First of two Derby dead-heats – Cadland beat The Colonel in a run-off. In 1884 St Gatien and Harvester's owners divided the stakes.

1845 . . . The first recorded Triple Dead Heat took place in the Glasgow Stakes Subscription Handicap at Newmarket on 30 October.

1851 . . . The Omnibus Stakes at The Hoo on 26 April produced the second ever Quadruple Dead Heat – Defaulter, Squire of Malton, Reindeer and Pulcherrina proved inseparable.

1855 . . . The last recorded Quadruple Dead Heat took place at Newmarket on 22 October with Overreach, Unexpected, Gamester and Lady Golightly proving impossible to separate.

1925 . . . The last recorded Triple Dead Heat in the Stayers Handicap at Folkestone on 5 September.

In 1965, Sea Bird II, often rated the best ever winner, was the 7/4 hero in Derby number **one hundred and eighty-six**. Trained in France.

1930 . . . For the last time in Britain a dead heat was run off as Ruby's Love beat Walloon at the second attempt in the Berks Selling Handicap at Newbury on 25 June.

1947 . . . Photo-finish camera introduced to British courses at Epsom on 22 April.

1949 . . . Photo-finish camera first used to decide the outcome of the Derby – Nimbus beat Amour Drake by a head.

1989 . . . 'Heads you lose, tails we win' at Oakley point to point meeting in Northamptonshire in June where, following a dead heat, the Tote returned stakes to those who had backed either 'winner' and kept all losing bets.

RACING QUOTES YOU SHOULDN'T EXPECT TO HEAR

'The Jockey Club was quite wrong' . . . David Pipe (Public defender of the Club)

'I hesitate to say this' . . . John McCririck (never short of an opinion)

'Keep the change' . . . legendary 'careful' Willie Carson

'Where's my white shirt, dear' . . . habitually red-clad Jack Berry

'As I was saying to my bookie pal' . . . Luca 'bookies are leeches' Cumani

'I've been invited to start the next National' . . . Captain Keith 'Cock-up' Brown

'I'm looking forward to commentating on Sunday racing' . . . Julian Wilson the ultimate anti-Sunday man

'My husband and I' . . . Jenny Pitman, former wife of jockey Richard

Willie Carson's highest seasonal winning total was
one hundred and eighty-seven in 1990.

'I've been a dope' . . . Frankie Dettori who once had a brief chat with the Constabulary about certain substances

'Come on, lads, it's about time we got together for a good old chin-wag' . . . the taciturn Lester Piggott

'He's tremendously well and can't get beat' . . . arch pessimist Tim Forster whose advice to his jockey once was 'keep remounting'

'A Tote monopoly is highly undesirable' . . . anti-bookie columnist Paul Haigh

'Tell those birds to clear off' . . . still fancied after all these years, John 'greatest jockey' Francome

SHERGAR SHAKE UP

1981 . . . Won Derby

1983 . . . Kidnapped – £2m ransom demanded. Never seen again.

1989 . . . *Sunday Sport* reported Shergar spotted on Dartmoor – being ridden by Lord Lucan.

1989 . . . 'Alive and well and has been on English soil' claimed American 'seer' Jeane Dixon in January edition of *Psychic News*.

1991 . . . 'Alive and grazing in a field in the Channel Islands' revealed the *Sun* in March.

1993 . . . 'Kidnapped to cover a hatful of very good mares. His pedigree lives on under another name' – fugitive punter and tipster, Hart Rogers speaks out in the *People*.

1994 . . . Woman with Irish accent calling herself Marli contacted bloodstock consultant David Horgan offering to reveal Shergar's whereabouts for £40,000. After several calls trail goes cold.

1994 . . . *Sunday Times* approached by gang wanting £20,000 for horse's remains.

Lester Piggott won the jockey title for the last time with **one hundred and eighty-eight** winners in 1982.

1994 . . . Part owner Stan Cosgrove told *Sporting Life* that former IRA man Sean O'Callaghan has given sworn affidavit that 'Shergar had gone berserk shortly after his abduction and been destroyed within hours of being taken'. Cosgrove believes Shergar buried 'in a bog in Aughnasheelan on the Leitrim-Fermanagh border'.

1996 . . . Ireland's RTE reported that a consortium of Dublin businessmen had arranged for Shergar's bones to be exhumed, and a deal was being arranged with Hollywood movie moguls.

1996 . . . DNA from two hairs taken as souvenirs from Shergar by students before his kidnap could prove conclusively whether any alleged remains are definitely those of Shergar, reported *The Times*.

FINANCIAL IRREGULARITIES

Spanish racing officials delayed handing over £57,000 prize money due to the Queen after the August 1993 victory of her Enharmonic at San Sebastian – because they said that for tax purposes they needed proof that the Queen was British.

In 1784 racing owners were up in arms about a new tax which it was proposed to introduce, of 'one guinea per annum and £5 on every winner'. It was eventually shelved.

Former jump jockey turned TV commentator Richard Pitman was once offered £1,200 to 'stop' Pendil. 'I stopped at once, looked the man in the eye and told him I was going to report him. He vanished immediately.'

Champion jockey Fred Archer was careful with money – a favourite trick was to ask for the loan of a few coins to put in his waistband to make up his weight – which he would then 'forget' to return.

The Rev John King, who died in 1875, was forced by his bishop to resign after his horse won the St Leger and he collected £15,000 in

---

Run on a Saturday for the first time in **one hundred and eighty-nine** years, Lochsong won the 1992 Ayr Gold Cup.

prize money during a single season's racing.

After Thomas Dawson had trained Ellington to win the 1856 Derby he left the £25,000 he won over the race in an old hat box on a luggage rack in a train on the way home. He advertised for the return of the box as containing 'nothing of interest' and got it back.

A jury awarded jockey Benito Narvaz 4.4 million dollars after ruling that officials at Tampa Bay downs in Florida were responsible for the 1990 fall which left him paralysed.

Manager of the Royal Stud, Richard, Earl of Stafford, received expenses of £10,000 – in 1730.

Christy Roche became the first jockey ordered to contribute towards the legal costs of an appeal hearing when, in July 1992, he was ordered to pay IR£5,000 to the Turf Club after losing his appeal against a 15-day riding ban.

The punter who had a standing order with his bookie to back Gordon Richards' main ride of the day to win £1,000 was a little miffed on 28 June, 1947, when Richards lost on 1-20 cert Glendower at Chepstow – costing him £20,000!

OLDIES BUT GOLDIES Racing's geriatrics!

83-year-old **Harry Beasley** rode unplaced Mollie in a flat race at Baldoyle, Dublin, in June 1935.

67-year-old **Victor Lawson** chalked up his first win in October 1973 on Ocean King, at Warwick.

31-year-old French-based stallion **Mystic** was still active during 1985.

Captain Cuttle became the oldest Derby winner on 31 May 1922, having been foaled on 11 January 1919.

Derby number **one hundred and ninety**, run in 1969, was won by 15/2 chance, Blakeney, ridden by Ernie Johnson, trained by Arthur Budgett.

October 1992's Belmont Park meeting saw 82-year-old Thomas Mellon Evans' **Pleasant Tap** win, along with 85-year-old Paul Mellon's **Sea Hero** and 95-year-old Fred Hooper's **Roman Envoy**.

31-year-old **Contract** gave birth to a filly in France in 1893.

22-year-old **Creggmore Boy** finished fourth at Cartmel in June 1962, the oldest recorded runner in a race.

18-year-old **Wild Aster** set a record by winning three times in 1919. **Sonny Somers** managed two at the same age in 1980.

15-year-old **Peter Simple** was the oldest Grand National winner (1853).

12-year-old **Silver Frame** (1951) and **What a Myth** (1969) are the oldest Cheltenham Gold Cup winners.

26-year-old **Muley** was the oldest sire of a Derby winner – Little Wonder, in 1840.

25-year-old **Horatia** was the oldest dam of a Derby Winner – Paris in 1806.

OUT ON A LIMB – BODILY ODDITIES

Frank Wise wore an artificial leg when riding Alike to win the 1929 Grand National.

Gerald Foljambe rode two jump winners at the Melton Hunt in 1925 despite having had a leg amputated below the knee.

Standing at the French National Stud in 1929, **Saint Hubert** savaged his groom, whose arm had to be amputated.

Sheila's Cottage won the 1948 Grand National then bit the top off of one of jockey Arthur Thompson's fingers.

Belper managed to win races despite having only one eye.

Eleven times champion jockey, Lester Piggott's most prolific season was 1966 when he won with a total of
one hundred and ninety-one winners.

Masked Ball was a winner – with only one testicle hence the name.

Prime Mover, a Southwell winner in 1993, did it with a hole where his left hip had once been.

A racegoer found himself with a broken nose – after criticizing US jockey **Alex Solis** who promptly cracked him with a left hander.

Owner **Tony McGuinness** celebrated as his Carramore Outlaw won for him – by falling over and breaking a bone in his back.

Rabelais, a 28-year-old French stallion, received the first ever penis transplant in an operation in 1928. It didn't work.

LETTERALLY AN A TO Z OF HORSE RACING MISCELLANY . . .

Alex Greaves, the first lady jockey to ride in the Derby – last on Portuguese Lily in 1996 – was described by champion jockey Frankie Dettori as 'an excellent rider and she has a wonderful pair of big breasts' on Channel 4's *Big Breakfast*.

Bullock – PC Alan, earned himself a commendation for bravery in May 1996 when he gambled with his own life to save jockey Adie Smith's at Cartmel racecourse. Smith's mount had fallen and he had been knocked out as he fell, and the fourteen other runners were jumping the fence where he lay. Bullock spread himself across the stricken jockey and the field somehow avoided them.

Carlton TV viewers were surprised to hear Jimmy Greaves comment, 'The Derby is only a race' during a June 1996 discussion about the world's greatest race.

Down – Alastair, of the *Sporting Life*, described the Cheltenham Festival as 'The most uncomfortable, expensive – and successful – sardine convention in the world'.

Geoff Lewis rode Mill Reef in Derby number **one hundred and ninety-two**, which was run in 1971. The pair won by two lengths.

Epsom's hallowed turf is threatened regularly – by people who scatter their loved-ones' ashes on the course. Groundsman Nigel Thornton groans 'Some secretly dump it – normally we put it in the earth behind the (winning) post.' It can affect grass growth.

'Fairie' Mr – the 'nom de course' under which early 20th-century Australian mining magnate A W Cox raced on the English turf – for reasons best known to himself, and almost certainly nothing to do with the fact that the horse with which he won the 1917 Derby was called Gay Crusader.

Gosforth Park races in Johannesburg had to be abandoned in October 1995 when racegoers rioted, following the disqualification of a well-backed favourite.

Heaviest flat jockeys listed in the 1996 edition of *Horses In Training* were T J Kent and V Smith, both weighing in at 10 stone.

Isle of Man's Douglas Racecourse staged its first meeting on 16 September 1869.

Jan Molby, former Liverpool soccer star turned manager, went into racehorse partnership with Ian Rush, owning Dajraan, and confessed to the *Racing Post*: 'I don't have many fun bets any more, and I'm making it pay these days – but it has been a bloody expensive learning process.'

Kelleway kapers and sniggers all round in August 1992 when jockey Bruce Raymond was suspended for interfering with Gay Kelleway's Night Gown – during a race at Folkestone.

Lightest flat jockey listed in 1996's *Horses in Training* was J F O'Reilly at 6st 3lbs.

Merseyside was the scene of a bizarre incident in November 1994 when 41-year-old George Rowe returned from a trip to his local betting shop to be told that he had been found dead in Thailand! Police finally discovered that his name had been 'borrowed' for a bogus passport found on an anonymous body.

One of racing's great finishes was witnessed in 1972 when Derby number **one hundred and ninety-three** was won by Lester Piggott and Roberto by a short head from Rheingold and Ernie Johnson.

13 November 1985 saw an odd event when air rifle pellets were fired at first aid officers at Wolverhampton racecourse where, despite attendance of just 180, the culprits were not apprehended.

On course bookmakers at Leopardstown went on strike twice during October 1995 in protest at the on-course betting shop being permitted to accept wagers on races at Leopardstown itself whilst the meeting was in progress.

Pascal Bary completed a unique Derby double within 45 minutes in June 1996 when his French Derby victory with his stable's Ragmar was rapidly followed by Arawak d'Aroco, also trained by the Frenchman, winning the French Arab Derby.

Q – 92 of the 16,3000 thoroughbreds listed in 1996's *Horses In Training* had names beginning with Q.

Robert Morley, actor, racing fan and racehorse owner, always had a clause written into his contracts that he would not do matinees on Derby days. He passed away aged 84 in 1992 – on Derby day.

Steve Donoghue, great champion jockey of the 1920s, was described thus by fellow rider Brownie Carslake: 'Stephen can find out more about what is left in his horse with his little finger than most men with their legs and whip.'

Tweseldown point-to-point meeting became the first course to race on a Sunday complete with on-course betting in January 1995 when a grey, Not Quite White, won the first race in front of a crowd of 4,000.

Unknown he may have been, but the owner of Our Home Land, who ran in Newcastle's Ramside Hall Hotel Stakes in May 1996, certainly attracted attention – after all, his name is Dr Fuk To Chang.

Vigilance became the first ever horse to be 'warned off' by the authorities for his own misdemeanours rather than those of his owners, in 1912, when he was debarred from future races 'on account of his savage propensities'.

Morston won the **one hundred and ninety-four**th Derby for trainer Arthur Budgett in 1973 just four years after he'd scored with Blakeney.

Winter, Fred, was interviewing a young hopeful called John Francome, for a job. Winter asked Francome 'What's the lightest you've ever been?' receiving the reply, 'Seven pounds four ounces.'

X – is the letter with which the names of just six of the 16,300 racehorses in training in 1996 began.

Yutaka Take, Japanese jockey, became the youngest rider – 26 – to complete 1,000 winning races when he rode Yale No Koibito to victory at Kookua on 23 July 1995.

Zorse racing could be big business in the future if recent experiments crossing horses with zebras prove successful.

ALPHA 'BETTING'
26 THINGS I'LL WAGER YOU NEVER KNEW ABOUT BETTING.

Anyone who enjoys a regular bet will tell you their first bet was a winning one – and that nowadays they break even – more or less!

Bogey – nothing to do with runny noses or bad golf-shots, it means the biggest loser in a bookie's list of liabilities.

Copped – don't call the police, this North Country slang expression means that the bookie has had a winning race.

Dodgepot – risky horse to back – combination of 'dodgy' and 'hotpot', generally a horse which can't be trusted to do its best.

Evens – or, slang, levels you devils. Betting odds of one to one – first recorded use in a 1632 play, *Hyde Park* by James Shirley.

Favourite – generally, but not always, the heaviest-backed runner in a race. Always the shortest-odds contender. Not quite as old a term as you might imagine – the first racing reference is from 1857.

Steve Cauthen notched up **one hundred and ninety-five** winners in 1985 to gain his second of three jockey titles..

Goliath – a bet for incurable optimists, consisting of 247 separate bets – 8 selections covered in 28 doubles, 56 trebles, 70 fourfolds, 56 fivefolds, 28 sixfolds, 8 sevenfolds and one eightfold. 'Named after its huge size, massive optimism and certain failure, said one cynic.

Hedging has very little to do with horticulture – it describes the way in which a bookmaker will reduce his own potential liability or pay-out by having a bet elsewhere himself.

If cash – term used when part of the returns from one wager are automatically reinvested on a subsequent bet.

Jolly – the jolly old favourite.

Killing – originally an Aussie term defined in 1919 as 'to win substantially from the bookmakers'.

Leg – originally a term for a bookmaker coined in the early 19th century as a shortened form of 'blackleg', which shows how good their reputation was then.

Macaroni – slang for the odds of 25/1.

Nap – a racing tipster's top selection – derived from the card game Napoleon in which to go nap is to win all five tricks. First recorded in a racing sense in 1884.

Odds – betting term for the price offered about a runner – first used, bizarrely enough, by one William Shakespeare in his *Henry IV*.

Pitch – dates from 1756 and describes the position where a bookmaker then known as a penciller and later as a metallician – would conduct his business on the racecourse.

Quotable betting quote: 'In betting on races, there are two elements that are never lacking: hope as hope, and an incomplete recollection of the past' . . . E V Lucas, *New York Times*, October 1951.

Rampers – described in the 1887 *Daily News* as 'men who claimed

On August 12 1991, Jim Bolger landed a **one hundred and ninety-six** and a half to one five timer from five runners at Gowran Park.

to have made bets to bookmakers, and hustled and surrounded them if they refused to pay'.

Sharp – backer of horses who manages to get hold of inside information. Not to be confused with your author's surname, of course, which possesses a final 'e' courtesy of his grandfather. Term first used in 1797.

Take – used as a verb by bookies to indicate a horse is odds-on – as in 'I'll take 7/4', which means the horse is actually offered at 4/7.

Up the arm – racecourse slang from tic tac, meaning 11/8 odds.

Value – that mystical ingredient sought by all punters – implies accepting odds which are higher than those the gambler believes to be appropriate.

Wrist – tic tac derived term for betting odds of 5/4. Also ideal for slapping when results go the wrong way.

X – alias frequently used by successful gamblers who would prefer not to be identified. Awkward when Mr X also happens to be their real name . . . admittedly an infrequent occurrence.

Yankee – common term for bet involving four selections in six doubles, four trebles and an accummulator. Name derived from 'Yankee tournament', a sporting event in which each competitor plays the others.

Zero – what the well-adjusted punter should anticipate receiving from his bookmaker – anything else then becomes a gratefully received bonus.

Hurdler, Indian Scene, won at Plumpton in March 1967, returning Tote odds of **one hundred and ninety-eight** to one.